*in the*
## AGE
*of the*
## PYRAMIDS

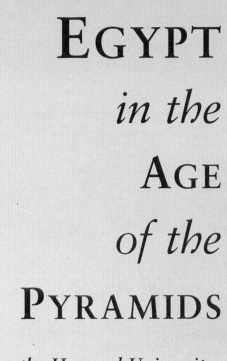

# EGYPT
## *in the*
# AGE
## *of the*
# PYRAMIDS

*Highlights from the Harvard University-
Museum of Fine Arts, Boston Expedition*

*Yvonne J. Markowitz*

*Joyce L. Haynes*

*Rita E. Freed*

**mfa**

MFA PUBLICATIONS
*a division of the*
Museum of Fine Arts, Boston

MFA Publications
*a division of the Museum of Fine Arts, Boston*
465 Huntington Avenue
Boston, Massachusetts 02115

Published in conjunction with the exhibition "Egypt in the Age of the Pyramids: Highlights from the Harvard University-Museum of Fine Arts Expedition," organized by the Museum of Fine Arts, Boston, in collaboration with the Nagoya/Boston Museum of Fine Arts in Nagoya, Japan. A slightly different version of this exhibition was shown at the Nagoya/Boston Museum of Fine Arts from September 15, 2001 to February 3, 2002.

Cincinnati Art Museum, Cincinnati, Ohio
March 18–June 16, 2002

Memphis Brooks Museum of Art, Memphis, Tennessee
February 25–May 18, 2003

Generous support for this publication was provided by the Andrew W. Mellon Publications Fund.

For a complete listing of MFA Publications, please contact the publisher at the above address, or call 617 369 3438.

Front cover: Triad of King Menkaure, the Goddess Hathor, and the Deified Hare Nome (cat. no. 5).

Back cover: Triad *in situ*, July 10, 1908 (fig. 9).

ISBN 0-87846-630-4

Library of Congress Card Number: 2001098092

Available through D.A.P. / Distributed Art Publishers
155 Sixth Avenue, 2nd floor
New York, New York 10013

Tel.: 212 627 1999 · Fax: 212 627 9484

FIRST EDITION
Printed and bound in Italy

# Contents

# Director's Foreword

Boston is home to one of the world's great collections of Egyptian art from the Age of the Pyramids. Excavated by the Harvard University-Museum of Fine Arts Expedition during the early decades of the twentieth century, it features signature works created over 4,500 years ago. The period, known as the Old Kingdom, was Egypt's crowning moment—a time when stone was fashioned into architectural marvels and the human figure was celebrated by superb statuary designed to last forever. The decorative arts also flourished, as evidenced by splendid furnishings, exquisite jewelry, and graceful stone vessels. The style is elegant but restrained, a reflection of an Egyptian ideal that became the standard for centuries to follow.

The scope and exceptional quality of the Egyptian collection at the Museum of Fine Arts, Boston, owes much to George Andrew Reisner, director of the Boston team at Giza and a pioneering force in the application of scientific methodology in archaeology. The extensive photographic and written records created in the field under his supervision are an integral part of the collection and a continuing resource for all those fascinated by this chapter in Egyptian history.

The Museum is pleased to share over a hundred objects from its permanent collection in an exhibition that reflects the epitome of Egyptian civilization during its first true blossoming.

MALCOLM ROGERS
*Ann and Graham Gund Director*
*Museum of Fine Arts, Boston*

# Acknowledgements

The encouragement and efforts of our colleagues at the Museum were evident from the project's inception. Katherine Getchell applied her extensive managerial abilities to the exhibition, and Gen Watanabe's superb organizational skills and diplomacy aided it at every step of the way. Thanks also go to Emily Lasner for her assistance and coordination of many details.

Our colleagues in the Art of the Ancient World, Lawrence Berman, Denise Doxey, Laura Gadbery, and Kaitlin Shinnick were always ready to lend their expertise and assistance at every level.

We appreciate the support of the entire staff of the Department of Conservation and Collections Management, headed by Arthur Beale. We are especially grateful to Objects Conservation under Pamela Hatchfield. Special thanks go to Abigail Hykin and C. Mei-An Tsu, who were responsible for the conservation and cleaning of 123 objects for this exhibition. Skillfully working with them was Susanne Gänsicke, Kent Severson, and Vanessa Tucom. In addition, we thank the conservators for sharing their insights on the ancient techniques used to create particular objects, thereby enhancing our understanding of these works of art. Richard Newman, Head of Scientific Research, spent many hours performing valuable scientific tests that enriched our knowledge of the collection and also advanced the understanding of Old Kingdom metallurgy. Jean-Louis Lachevre, along with George Hagerty, performed extraordinary feats in preparing steel mounts for the large stone objects for display and shipping. Gordon Hanlon, Head of Furniture and Frame Conservation, oversaw the cleaning and restoration of the Hetepheres furniture ensemble, bringing a new gleam to the already spectacular furniture. Thanks also to Nadia Lokma, Chief Conservator from the Cairo Museum, for her valuable insights on the assembly of the Hetepheres furniture.

We appreciate the careful restoration of inscribed textile fragments from a mummy and assistance with the beadnet dress project by Meredith Montague of Textiles and Costumes Conservation. Thanks go to Sheila Shear for her research, expertise, and infinite patience in reconstructing the dress. Jessie Ring and Harriet Heyman assisted her in the sorting of the beads. Hamdy Monem Abdel Mohamed performed the painstaking cleaning of the ancient beads. Also, thanks to Millicent Jick for her useful information, support, and encouragement in this endeavor. Herbie Johnson lent his fine craftsmanship by making the frames for the beadnet dress assembly.

We thank Collections Care Specialists Karen Gausch, Will Jeffers, Seth Waite, and Garrick Manninen for mounting the objects for exhibition in such a way that the artwork is enhanced and protected.

The unsurpassed expertise of the Museum's Photography Studio make this catalogue a visual delight and we express thanks to Tom Lang, John Woolf, Damon Beale, Gary Ruuska, and Saravuth Neou. Our very special appreciation goes to Greg Heins, who graciously addressed all our individual visual concerns.

We are grateful to Emiko Usui for her patience and careful scrutiny of this manuscript, as well as to Sarah McGaughey for the thorough editorial work. Cynthia Randall created the book's fine design and also managed the production with the assistance of Dacey Sartor. We are indebted to Mark Polizzotti for moving forward with an English version of this catalogue and recognizing that it would be a useful scholarly addition to the Museum's publications.

Many thanks go to the members of the Registrar's Office for overseeing the complex details of the loan and the packing of the objects. They include Patricia Loiko, Tsugumi Maki Joiner, Kim Pashko, Julia McCarthy, Adelia Bussey, and Mary Lister.

We are indebted to the experts of the Paper Conservation Department, including Roy Perkinson, Annette Manick, Gail English, and Consultant Paper Conservator Elizabeth Coombs for cleaning and mounting our letter to the dead.

For the coordination of images and preparation of prints and chromes, we are grateful to members of the Department of Visual Archives, including Jennifer Riley, Angela Segalla, Kristen Bierfelt, and Erika Field.

We would like to give special thanks for the many references, suggestions, and assistance in finding archival material to Peter Der Manuelian, Research Fellow of the Andrew Mellon Giza Archives Project. His expertise and knowledge of Giza mastaba tombs was invaluable. He also created excellent maps and graphics for this publication. The catalogue has also benefited tremendously from the scrutiny of Ann Macy Roth, who read the manuscript, made many insightful comments, and gave her expert advice. We would like to thank Peter Lacovara for lending his expertise and taking time to answer many queries. Diane Flores, Research Associate of the Andrew Mellon Giza Archives Project, was extremely helpful in locating glass plate negatives of objects and work in progress from George Reisner's excavations. Also, we are grateful to John Nolan, Assistant Field Director for the Giza Plateau Mapping Project, who shared his recent findings on Old Kingdom cylinder seals and impressions.

We would like to thank Joseph A. Greene and James Armstrong of the Semitic Museum of Harvard University for graciously loaning objects that were part of the Semitic Museum installation on Giza.

Our many volunteers eased the workload of this project by giving their time and energy. We would like to thank Margy Faulkner and Meg Robbins for their careful and painstaking work on the bibliography. Libby Mottur and Nancy McMahon also gave valuable assistance.

YVONNE J. MARKOWITZ
JOYCE L. HAYNES
RITA E. FREED

# Chronology of Ancient Egypt

| | |
|---|---|
| **Predynastic Period** | 4800–3100 B.C. |
| **Dynasty 0** | 3100–3000 B.C. |
| **Early Dynastic Period** | 3000–2675 B.C. |

**Old Kingdom**

| | |
|---|---|
| Dynasty 3 | 2675–2625 B.C. |

At least five kings, including Djoser, Sekhemkhet, and Huni

Dynasty 4

| | |
|---|---|
| Sneferu | 2625–2585 B.C. |
| Khufu (Cheops) | 2585–2560 B.C. |
| Redjedef (Djedefre) | 2560–2555 B.C. |
| Khafre (Chephren) | 2555–2532 B.C. |
| Menkaure (Mycerinus) | 2532–2510 B.C. |
| Wehemka? | 2510–2508 B.C. |
| Shepseskaf | 2508–2500 B.C. |

Dynasty 5

| | |
|---|---|
| Userkaf | 2500–2485 B.C. |
| Sahure | 2485–2472 B.C. |
| Neferirkare Kakai | 2472–2462 B.C. |
| Shepseskaf/Reneferef | 2462–2455 B.C. |
| Nyuserre | 2455–2425 B.C. |
| Menkauhor | 2425–2415 B.C. |
| Djedkare Isesi | 2415–2371 B.C. |
| Unas | 2371–2350 B.C. |

Dynasty 6

| | |
|---|---|
| Teti | 2350–2338 B.C. |
| Meryre Pepy I | 2338–2298 B.C. |
| Merenre (Nemtyemzaf) | 2298–2288 B.C. |
| Neferkare Pepy II | 2288–2194 B.C. |

Rulers including

| | |
|---|---|
| Queen Nitocris | 2194–2170 B.C. |
| Dynasties 7–8 | 2170–2130 B.C. |

An undetermined number of monarchs ruling from Memphis

| | |
|---|---|
| **First Intermediate Period** | 2130–1980 B.C. |
| **Middle Kingdom** | 1980–1630 B.C. |
| **Second Intermediate Period** | 1630–1539 B.C. |
| **New Kingdom** | 1539–1075 B.C. |
| **Third Intermediate Period** | 1075–656 B.C. |
| **Late Period** | 664–332 B.C. |
| **Greco-Roman Period** | 332 B.C.–A.D. 642 |

Based on William J. Murnane, "The History of Ancient Egypt," in *Civilizations of the Ancient Near East*, ed. Jack M. Sasson (New York, 1995), 2:712–14.

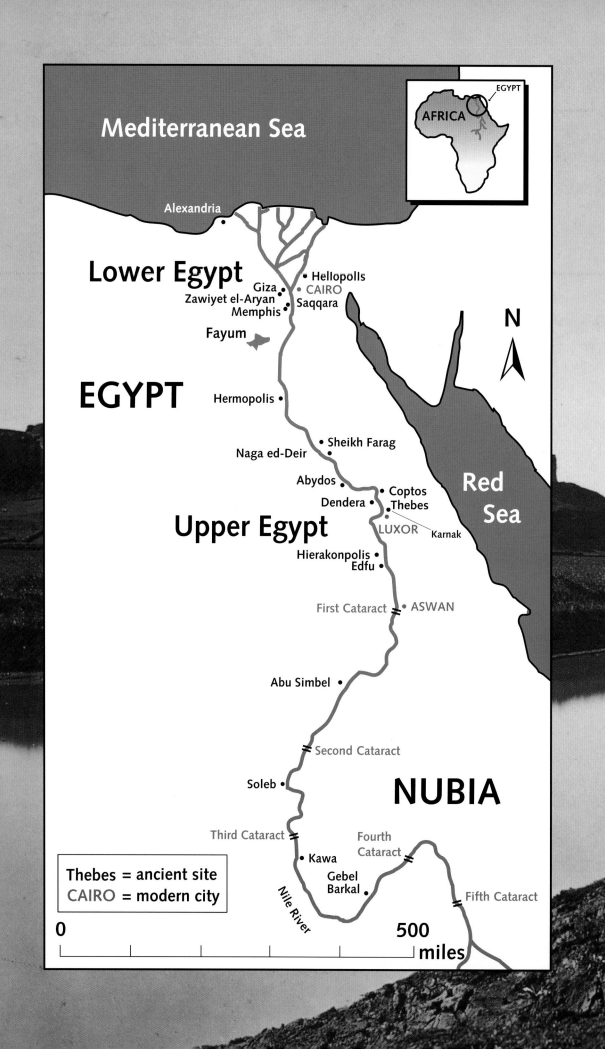

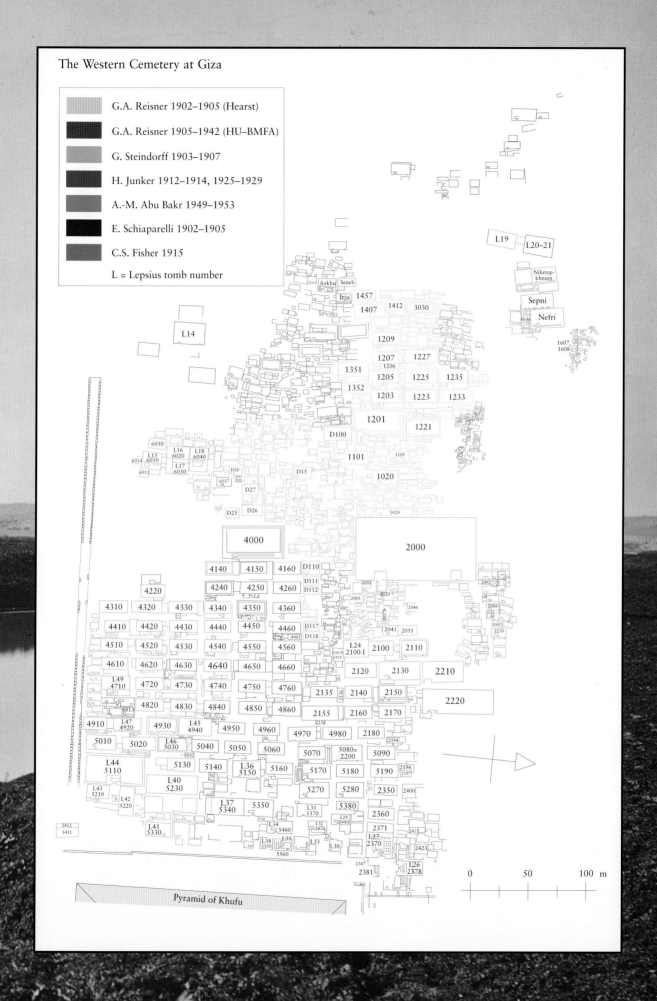

The Western Cemetery at Giza

# Egypt in the Age of the Pyramids

**RITA E. FREED**

Of all the monuments created by man, few have attracted as much attention or earned as much respect as the pyramids of Egypt. Designed to protect and preserve the body of the king so that he might enjoy eternal life, they became international tourist attractions shortly after they were built, and to this day they engender awe and admiration for the culture that created them 4,500 years ago. They are products of a golden age that later Egyptian dynasties actively, but unsuccessfully, attempted to emulate. The civilization of the Pyramid Age with its three basic tiers—kings, bureaucrats, and common workers—represents a high point in cultural development and forms the topic of this special exhibition.

The Pyramid Age, also called the Old Kingdom (2675–2130 B.C.), evolved from well over a thousand years of cultural development in the Nile Valley. With the gradual desiccation of the Sahara region, the Nile River invited permanent settlements, which grew in size, social organization, and material goods during the fourth millennium B.C. The river not only provided a reliable source of water, but also left behind a layer of fertile silt in which crops could easily be grown following its annual flooding. By about 3000 B.C., population centers along the Nile from the Mediterranean south to at least the first cataract at Aswan shared a common culture and were united under the umbrella of a single ruler often identified as Narmer.[1] Narmer became the first king of Egypt's 1st Dynasty. Egypt's first two dynasties are now known as the Early Dynastic Period (3000–2675 B.C.).[2]

The monuments of Narmer make it clear that the foundations of Egyptian art, architecture, and culture were already in place by Dynasty 1. On a large ceremonial macehead, for example, an early king excavates a canal and thereby controls the waters of the Nile (fig. 1). The crown and garment he wears, including the bull's tail tied at his waist, label him as king—these symbols would identify monarchs for the remainder of Egyptian dynastic history and beyond. Even at this early date, reality bowed to propaganda as the king's height was made to dwarf that of his attendants. His one-foot-forward stance and combination of profile and frontal views likewise became synonymous with Egyptian relief representation.

Greywacke statue of
King Menkaure and a queen,
Dynasty 4 (detail).

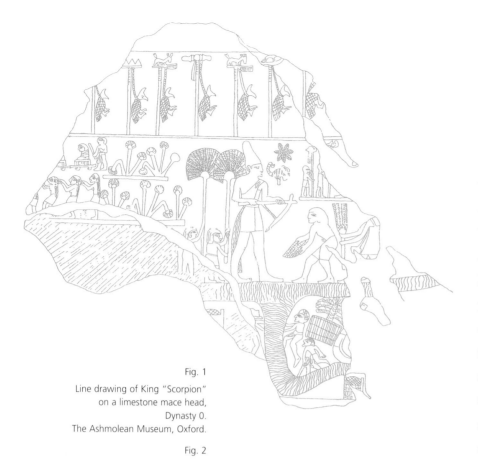

Fig. 1

Line drawing of King "Scorpion"
on a limestone mace head,
Dynasty 0.
The Ashmolean Museum, Oxford.

Fig. 2

Colossal limestone statue of Min
from Coptos, Dynasty 0.
The Ashmolean Museum, Oxford.

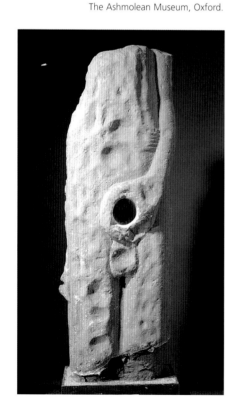

At the time of the unification of the country, many cultural landmarks were achieved. Most importantly, a written language developed from pictograms with a few alphabetic signs into a syllabary with complex grammatical forms. Writing was now used to label, number, and describe people and commodities. Later it would be used for narrative purposes as well. In the sculptural arts, artists grew accustomed to working in the round in addition to two-dimensional relief. Their struggle to liberate organic forms from the stone matrix became ever more successful as they rendered first animal and then human figures naturalistically. Some of the earliest sculpture represents divinities whose size and awesome majesty bespoke their control over the universe (fig. 2). Temples established for the worship of such divinities continued as holy places in enlarged and elaborated forms for millennia.[3]

Many of the great urban centers of the Pyramid Age were already thriving in the Early Dynastic Period according to both tradition and the archaeological record. Of these areas, much is still buried under later remains. Such is fortunately not the case with necropoli, cemeteries that were situated in the desert outside urban and agricultural areas. There, rulers expended considerable energy to build massive tombs in order to ensure the preservation of their bodies. Located at Abydos in Upper Egypt, and later at Saqqara at the juncture of the Delta and Nile Valley, these consisted of roofed underground burial chambers and separately constructed superstructures.[4] At Saqqara, the superstructures took the form of rectangular buildings, called *mastabas*, with niched facades. They could either be solid inside or contain a series of progressively smaller rectangles resembling steps.[5] At Abydos, in addition to the tomb, separate enclosures as large as 100 by 55 meters were built closer to the Nile Valley's edge and presumably served as staging areas for funerary rites. Mudbrick was the primary building material for all of these constructions.

Because it was believed that the body would be rejuvenated and enjoy a blissful eternity if certain conditions were met, tombs of kings and high officials were equipped with items considered necessary for the afterlife. These included food and drink in appropriate stone and ceramic vessels (thousands at times!), beds, chests, jewelry for personal adornment, games for amusement, and ritual goods. At first servants were sacrificed and buried in subsidiary tombs within royal enclosures, but by the end of Dynasty 1 this custom was abandoned.

Although the king himself was not worshipped as a god at this time, the office of kingship was considered divine. The king's power, both real and magical, and the artist's ability to render it by the end of the Early Dynastic Period are shown by a statue of Khasekhem (fig. 3), one of a pair erected in the temple at Hierakonpolis. The king wears the crown of Upper Egypt and an enveloping cloak, signifying that he has just performed the jubilee (*heb-sed*) ceremony of rejuvenation that guaranteed him millions of years of rule. Awkward proportions, a thick neck, and limbs stiffly clinging to the body show the artist's lack of expertise in executing human sculpture on a large scale. Yet the subtle modeling of the eye and cheek focus attention on the head and show an ability to render detail in a naturalistic manner. An inscription on the base of the companion statue alludes to the king's worldly power in overcoming internal struggles. A speared and bound figure wearing a papyrus headdress of Lower Egypt lies beside other fallen captives whose number—47,209—is prominently displayed on the front!

In nearly every way, the Early Dynastic Period provided the cultural, economic, and philosophical building blocks for the Pyramid Age, or Old Kingdom. The Old Kingdom was a prosperous era of approximately five hundred years (2675–2130 B.C.) beginning with Dynasty 3 and continuing through Dynasty 8. Recent excavations have provided substantial information about the Old Kingdom's domestic, administrative, and religious establishments, although as before, funerary material remains a primary source of knowledge about these areas. Challenges to royal authority as alluded to in the Khasekhem statue seem to have been overcome by Dynasty 3, and the authority of the king became absolute. Power was centered in the Memphite area, which included the necropoli at Saqqara, Giza, Abusir, and Abu Roash.

Fig. 3
Schist statue of King Khasekhem, Dynasty 2.
The Egyptian Museum, Cairo.

## PYRAMIDS AND ROYAL SCULPTURE

Mastabas with internal steps may have provided the inspiration for the next stage in the evolution of funerary structures, seen in King Djoser's Step Pyramid of Dynasty 3 (fig. 4). The Step Pyramid is not only the first large-scale stone structure in the world, but also one of the most beautiful. It is thought to replicate, in a permanent material, components of his mudbrick palace complex in nearby Memphis, Egypt's capital. A series of enlargements transformed it

Fig. 4
The Step Pyramid of King Djoser at Saqqara, Dynasty 3.

Fig. 5
The Bent Pyramid of King Sneferu at Dahshur, Dynasty 4.

from a simple rectangular mastaba to a soaring, six-stepped edifice. Perishable materials employed earlier such as mudbrick, timber, and reeds were now imitated in limestone and *faience*, a self-glazing material composed of quartz, lime, and alkali. Beneath, corridors stretching an amazing three and a half miles connected four hundred rooms—an eloquent testimony to both architectural prowess and the king's ability to command the resources to build and equip such a labyrinth.[6] (Robbed in antiquity, the thieves nevertheless left behind an estimated forty thousand stone vessels.) Outside, a 10.4 meter high niched wall of stone enclosed an area of approximately 15 hectares, inside of which, in addition to the pyramid, were structures relating to the jubilee ceremony that guaranteed the renewal of his kingship. Other aspects of the pyramid also addressed its religio-magic function, including fourteen false gateways around the pyramid's perimeter, a second structure that replicates aspects of the king's underground tomb chambers, a large-scale representation of the king to house his soul, or *ka*, and an altar to which offerings for consumption by the king in the afterlife might be brought.

The evolution from step pyramid to true pyramid was a rapid one. Several 3rd Dynasty successors of Djoser's attempted step pyramids but died before their completion. The first true pyramids date to the reign of the first king of Dynasty 4, Sneferu, who actually built a total of three large pyramids in the course of his fifty-year rule.[7] All were in the vicinity of the capital, Memphis. Sneferu began the earliest one at Meidum as a step pyramid, but at the end of his reign, he added a smooth, straight-sided casing, thereby converting it to a true pyramid. Sneferu's second pyramid (fig. 5), now known as the Bent

Fig. 6

The pyramids at Giza, looking
northwest, April 24, 1999.

Pyramid at Dahshur, was built as a true pyramid with a steep slope of approximately 60 degrees. When the pyramid was enlarged, construction problems forced a reduction of the slope first to about 55 degrees and then finally to 43 degrees. This change gave the structure its unusual shape. There and in most later pyramids at Giza and elsewhere, chambers were constructed within the pyramid itself rather than beneath as before. Sneferu's third and final pyramid, most likely the one in which he was buried,[8] conforms to a manageable 43 degree slope throughout. For his pyramids and associated mortuary temples, it has been estimated that Sneferu moved an unbelievable 3.6 million cubic meters of stone—at least a million more than any king before or after.[9]

It was Khufu, Sneferu's son and successor, who selected the Giza plateau as the site for his funerary establishment and built the first and largest pyramid there. His monument is known today as the Great Pyramid (fig. 6, far right). Scholars estimate that builders used 2,300,000 limestone blocks for this structure that once soared to a height of 146.6 meters.[10] It was situated just a few feet short of true north, an orientation shared by several of the internal corridors. This orientation was thought to have facilitated the king's afterlife journey to join the circumpolar stars in the heavens.

The pyramid was but one element of Khufu's mortuary complex. The complex also included a temple only recently discovered at the edge of the flood plain (valley temple), a causeway connecting that temple to another adjacent to the pyramid's east side (pyramid temple), and an enclosure wall setting off the sacred ground. Each element in what was to become the classical pyramid complex layout either played a role (as yet poorly understood) in the ceremonies connected with preparation of the king's body for burial and rebirth, or replicated on a small scale the king's palace.[11] Tantalizing fragments of relief make it clear that the walls of these 4th Dynasty structures were decorated (cat. no. 11).

Near the Great Pyramid were three small pyramids for Khufu's queens and possibly his mother, Hetepheres (cat. nos. 1–2),[12] seven pits for boats used in the transport of the king's funerary entourage or to facilitate his travel in the afterlife, and mastabas neatly laid out in streets to the east (Eastern Cemetery) and west (Western Cemetery) for the king's close family and highest officials. By the next reign, further out, behind a wall, the support structures necessary to sustain an undertaking of this magnitude were constructed, including bakeries, breweries, storage magazines, and administrative buildings.[13] The houses and tombs of some of the estimated 25,000 laborers who built the pyramid complex were also nearby.

The pyramid establishments of Khufu's son, Khafre, and grandson, Menkaure, followed the same basic layout as Khufu's, although they were smaller. In addition, the preserved statuary of the king in the temple has a timeless appeal and an unsurpassed beauty. (Khufu's mortuary temples probably once housed statues as well, but to date, none have been found.) As surrogates for the king's body, such statues were intended to receive food offerings and served as resting places for his soul.

A seated statue of Khafre (fig. 7), the best preserved of twenty-three that originally stood in his valley temple, shows how much Egyptian artists had progressed since the Early Dynastic Period. No longer hesitant about carving stone, they now exploited it to perfection and even sought out exotic types. The Khafre statue is made of anorthosite gneiss, a variegated hard stone quarried in the Western Desert of Nubia. With its broad shoulders, taught muscles, and ageless, transcendent gaze, it eloquently expresses the Egyptian ideal of kingship and its connection to the divine, a concept reinforced by the falcon, whose outstretched wings embrace and protect the king's head. The falcon represents Horus, the god of kingship. In this instance, Horus is shown zoomorphically. He, like many other deities, may also be shown with a human body and animal head.

The statue of Menkaure and a queen (fig. 8) from that king's valley temple represents the achievement of the same ideal in standing group statuary. Both king and queen look beyond the viewer, out of the here and now into a timeless eternity. Menkaure's perfectly formed, athletic body exhibits no sign of age or infirmity. His queen, with her slender torso emphasized by a clinging garment, articulates feminine beauty. Although the queen's arms embrace Menkaure, no human emotion is expressed. These were the concepts private statuary imitated but rarely achieved (cat. no. 27). The king's forward left foot conveys a sense of motion, although in contrast to Greek sculpture his weight remains on his rear foot. Most often females stand with both feet together, but this queen's left foot is slightly forward.

Despite the number and quality of sculptures found in Menkaure's mortuary temples (cat. nos. 6, 7), his pyramid, at a mere 64.9 meters in height, was considerably smaller than those of his two predecessors.[14] This trend towards placing increased emphasis on the mortuary temples would continue in Dynasties 5 and 6 with the pyramid complexes at Saqqara and Abusir.[15] In Dynasty 5, rulers also erected temples to the sun close to their pyramids.

Abundant relief decoration survives from the pyramid complexes of Dynasty 5 and 6. Beginning with the reign of Unas, the last king of Dynasty 5, inscriptions on the inside of pyramids, now known as "Pyramid Texts," presented a series of magical spells to insure the king's deification and well-being in the afterlife.[16] Themes from these texts carved on the walls of pyramid temples, causeways, and valley temples highlighted the king's prowess, illustrated his role in maintaining order in the universe, demonstrated his closeness to the gods, and provided sustenance for his afterlife. Occasionally, they even seemed to refer to a specific event such as a famine in the reign of Unas (fig. 36, p. 73), or the placing of Sahure's pyramid capstone. Another scene in Sahure's pyramid temple depicts the conquest and imminent execution of a Libyan ruler, whose family begs Sahure for leniency. While this may have been a historic event of Sahure's reign, it certainly was not the case during the reign of Pepy II of Dynasty 6, who copied his predecessor's scenes to the point of including the names of the Libyans![17]

No discussion of the pyramids would be complete without a mention of the sphinx, located due east of Khafre's pyramid. A natural outcropping of rock was shaped, most believe, during the reign of Khafre to resemble the head of the reigning monarch and the body of a lion.[18] Almost every subsequent ruler would represent himself (or herself) as a sphinx, an icon of power that became synonymous with kingship. In the New Kingdom more than a millennium later, the great sphinx at Giza was deified and worshipped as Harmachis, a form of the sun god.

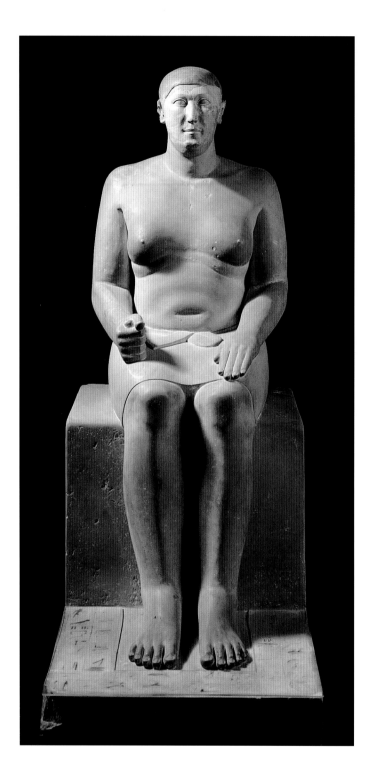

Fig. 9

Limestone figure of Hemiunu, Dynasty 4, reign of Khufu. Roemer- und Pelizaeus-Museum, Hildesheim.

## LIFE DURING THE PYRAMID AGE

The structure of Egyptian society has often been compared to a pyramid, with the king at the apex, the bureaucratic class made up of the king's trusted officials in the middle, and farmers and other laborers making up the broad base. Estimates place the population of Egypt in the Old Kingdom at about two million, although only the smallest fraction of those numbered among the official class and left records.[19] Most information about these people and how they lived comes from their funerary remains, particularly from the relief and paintings that decorated tomb walls. Substantial towns of the Old Kingdom have been excavated at Elephantine and Ayn-Asil in the Dakhleh Oasis, both remote from the Memphite area. These towns were protected by substantial mudbrick walls and included densely packed houses, administrative buildings, industrial areas, crafts workshops, and temples to local deities.[20]

Just as pyramids and their associated structures provide most of our information about kings and kingship in the Old Kingdom, burial places that surrounded each pyramid for the king's elite supply a wealth of information about daily life, including family structure, clothing, food and drink, occupations, and leisure activities. At times mimicking the layout of royal funerary establishments, they could reach an enormous size.[21] Substantial numbers of private tombs were also located in provincial centers, particularly during the later Old Kingdom.

Statuary and relief indicate that Egyptian men married one wife at a time and were proudly represented for eternity with their spouses and children. Depictions rarely provide reliable indicators of age, for just as kings were depicted in the prime of youth with perfect bodies, so too were most officials and their wives. The occasional corpulence in a man signified maturity and prosperity (fig. 9). Generally faces as well were idealized, although a few exceptions demonstrate that artists were capable of superb portraiture when called upon to produce it. The bust of Ankhhaf (fig. 10), for example, depicts not just any stern and capable man but a distinct indi-

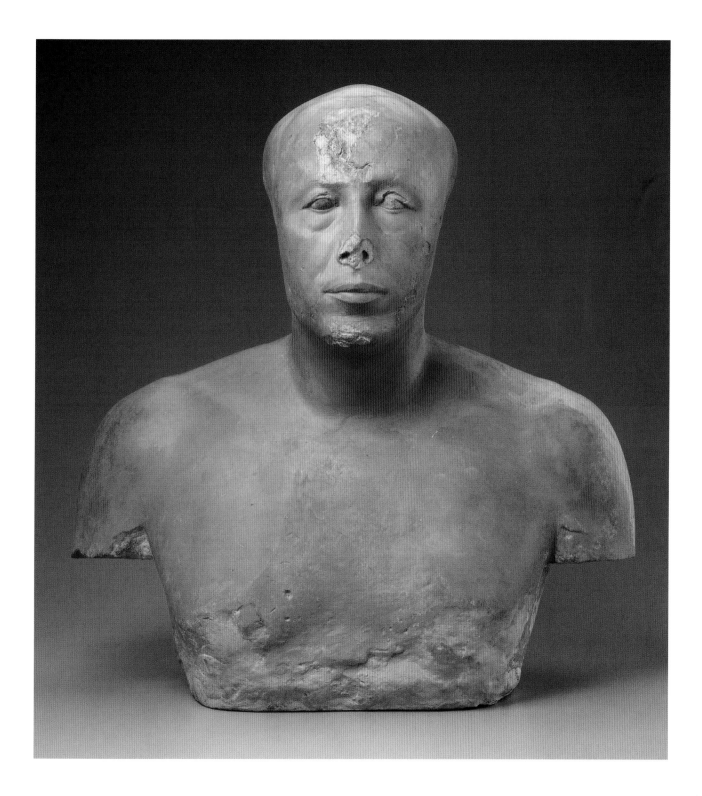

Fig. 10
Painted limestone bust of
Prince Ankhhaf, Dynasty 4,
reign of Khafre.

vidual. Children up until adolescence were shown with chubby, androgynous bodies, naked, with their right index finger touching their lips and their hair arranged in a single side lock (fig. 11).

Although in their depictions adult women wear tight-fitting, sleeveless sheath dresses, rare surviving examples of ancient Egyptian garments are pleated and have sleeves (fig. 12). All are made of undyed linen. Men wore wrapped kilts that varied in length from knee to shin. In tomb relief and on statuary, most garments were painted white. Beaded broadcollars (cat. nos. 37–38), chokers (cat. no. 18), bracelets (cat. no. 37), and anklets made of faience, semiprecious stones, or even gold added color and interest. Both men and women seem to have kept their natural hair short and wore wigs for festive occasions. Male laborers occasionally wore no clothes, as the task warranted.

Although just how many meals Egyptians of the Pyramid Age consumed each day is not known, what they ate is known, thanks to food remains and their depictions on tomb walls. Scenes frequently also show farming (fig. 13) and food preparation. Wheat and barley were staples whose harvest was recorded and taxed. The king's share was stored in granaries for distribution to those who worked for him, or made into bread and beer for the gods. King Sahure of Dynasty 5, for example, awarded the goddess Nekhbet of Upper Egypt eight hundred portions of bread and beer daily, while Wadjet of Lower Egypt received 4,800![22] (It would have been redistributed once the deities had their fill.) Pyramid workers also consumed beer and bread prepared in a bakery that was recently discovered at the south end of the Giza plateau.[23] This diet was augmented by fish that was also processed nearby. In addition to these foods, fowl trapped in the marshes and a variety of vegetables probably made up most of the diet of the average Egyptian.

The elite class in their ideal existence as recorded in their tombs fared much better than the pyramid workers. Some tombs contain a detailed menu for eternity. Niankhnesut, for example, in his tomb at Giza lists nineteen varieties of bread and cake, ten types of beef, seven kinds of fruit, four different sorts of fowl, but just one vegetable (onions). To drink, he included beer represented by seven different brews and two types of wine.[24]

The king granted land to the officials who served him, and these properties were not only large but also included a substantial work force. Activities on a large estate typically included farming, animal husbandry, viticulture, food preparation, and manufacturing, and every stage in each of these activities was carved or painted on tomb walls. In order for the same Niankhnesut mentioned above to insure he had what he needed, his estate employed five butlers, three butchers, two bakers, and a cook. There were, in addition, eleven scribes, two dining room directors, two overseers of linen, one seal bearer,

and a director of workers. All of this was the responsibility of two estate overseers.[25] Royal estates, temples, and the necropolis had respective activities also presided over by long lists of officials, which grew in number as the Old Kingdom progressed. In all, the nearly four thousand known titles and epithets for bureaucrats of the Pyramid Age illustrate the complexity of its administration and social organization.[26]

Although remains of actual workshops are few, tomb reliefs provide valuable insights into industries and manufacturing techniques of the time. The tomb of the 5th Dynasty overseer of pyramids, Ti, at Saqqara is particularly rich and informative. Detailed scenes feature potters, sculptors, stone vessel makers, carpenters, ship builders, leather workers, seal makers, metalsmiths, and mat makers engaged in their craft. Texts above each scene either describe it or capture the workers' conversation. A carpenter, for example, advises his colleague using a saw, "Take another! It is hot!"[27] This and similar scenes demonstrate that wood was cut by lashing it to an upright pole and pulling a saw through it (fig. 14). Awls, axes, adzes, mallets, bow drills, and a variety of chisels (cat. no. 41) made up the woodworker's toolbox in addition to saws. These items are not only depicted on walls, but also found in tombs and workshops. Presumably most of the products being made in Ti's reliefs were intended for his tomb. In another scene from the same tomb, extra goods are bartered in the market. (Coinage did not exist in Egypt until millennia later.)

Although life for the average Egyptian of the Pyramid Age was

Fig. 13

Agricultural relief scene from the offering chapel of Sekhemankhptah, Dynasty 5.

Fig. 14

Line drawing of the pull saw scene from the tomb of Ti at Saqqara, Dynasty 6.

Fig. 15

Boat jousting scene from the offering chapel of Sekhemankhptah, Dynasty 5.

undoubtedly difficult, tomb scenes also show interludes of fun, particularly for children. According to these scenes, male children played leapfrog and wrestled. They also engaged in various acrobatic feats. Adult men used sticks to wrestle or joust from boats (fig. 15). Much tamer were board games where playing pieces were moved across a board shaped like a rectangle or coiled snake. A different type of amusement was provided by musicians, singers, and dancers. The tomb of Niankhkhnum and Khnumhotep at Saqqara includes an ensemble of eleven, including two harps, two flutes, one clarinet, and six singers or so-called "chironomists" whose hand gestures may also have served to conduct or guide the musicians in what notes to play.[28] Dancers frequently accompanied musicians. Workers sang as they toiled, and although time has not preserved their melodies, it has preserved their words:

*Where is the one skilled at his job?*
*It is I!*[29]

## EPILOGUE

After more than five hundred years of stability and prosperity, what brought an end to the Pyramid Age? In all likelihood, the reasons were multiple and complex. Several hundred years of pyramid building taxed resources and generated no income. Over time, the king appointed and supported an ever-growing number of bureaucrats, and this placed an additional drain on the country's coffers. Further, institutions such as temples were granted tax exemptions (cat. no. 21). During times of prosperity and optimism, the country coped. Belief in the king's absolute power, however, was challenged by a series of inadequate Nile floods that brought famine and perhaps even attacks from desert raiders. Particularly toward the end of King Pepy II's long reign that lasted an unbelievable ninety-four years, the king appears not to have been able to bring relief. He was succeeded by a series of rulers, including one queen, who held power for only a few years, and the country fragmented. The production of sculpture and relief diminished greatly both in quantity and quality, because there were no longer ample resources to support it (fig. 16). Provincial centers answered to their own rulers, and no central authority had the strength to challenge them. An overall pessimism had set in. Egypt had entered the First Intermediate Period.

Fig. 16
Limestone statuette of a seated man, Dynasty 6.

NOTES

1. Narmer may be the same person as Menes on later king lists. For an overview of this problem, see Brewer and Teeter 1999, 32–33.

2. Manetho, the Greek historian who lived during the time of Ptolemy II (285–246 B.C.), first divided Egyptian history into dynasties. It is this system that is followed today, although in many instances, including the transition from Dynasty 2 to 3, the reason for changing dynasties remains unknown. See Hornung 1999, 13.

3. One such example is a temple to the goddess Satet on Elephantine. First established in the Early Dynastic Period, it was enlarged or rebuilt repeatedly through the Ptolemaic Period (332–30 B.C.). See Kaiser 1998, 283–87.

4. For a recent overview of the location and development of the Early Dynastic Period's royal tombs, see Seidelmayer 1998, 30ff.

5. Dynasty 1, reign of Azib (circa 2800 B.C.), illustrated in Smith 1998, 19, fig. 22.

6. For these and other amazing statistics, see Lehner 1997, 84ff.

7. In addition, he built a small step pyramid at Seila. See Lehner 1997, 96.

8. Lehner 1997, 105.

9. Stadelmann 1998, 57.

10. Lehner 1997, 108.

11. Lehner 1997, 27.

12. Stadelmann 1998, 64.

13. Lehner 1997, 236–37.

14. Lehner calculated that Menkaure's pyramid was only one-tenth the building mass of his grandfather Khufu's; see Lehner 1997, 135.

15. Stadelmann 1998, 70.

16. Robins 1997, 58–62.

17. It is further interesting to note that this very scene, including the Libyan names, also was copied about 1,500 years later at Kawa in the Sudan during the reign of Taharqa. For the differences between Sahure's original concepts and Pepy II's copies, see Dorothea Arnold 1999, 96–97.

18. For another view that dates the sphinx to the reign of Khufu, see Stadelmann 1998, 73–75.

19. Stadelmann 1998, 66.

20. For Elephantine, see Kaiser 1998, 283–85. For Ayn-Asil, see Soukiassian, Wuttmann, and Schaad 1990, 348–51. Other Old Kingdom settlements existed throughout the Nile Valley and Delta, but less is known about them. See Wenke et al. 1988.

21. The 5th Dynasty tomb of Ptahshepses at Abusir encompassed an area of 80 by 107 meters. See Jánosi 1999, 34. The funerary chapel of the Dynasty 6 vizier Mereruka and his family consisted of thirty-two relief-decorated rooms! See Altenmüller 1998, 79.

22. Breasted 1906, 159.

23. Lehner 1997, 236–37.

24. Málek 1986, 44.

25. Lehner 1997, 231.

26. Jones 2000, 2:1017, positively identifies 3,765. A number of the titles seem to have been honorary and without real responsibilities.

27. Málek 1986, 56.

28. Manniche 1991, 30–32.

29. Manniche 1991, 17.

# Excavating Giza

**YVONNE J. MARKOWITZ**

When George Andrew Reisner (fig. 17) became director of the Harvard University-Museum of Fine Arts, Boston, Expedition to Egypt in 1905, he already held excavation rights at Giza. The site, located southwest of modern Cairo and the ancient capital city of Memphis, served as a burial place for Egypt's mighty 4th Dynasty rulers, their relatives and functionaries, and a number of leading officials of the 5th and 6th Dynasties. Although Giza is best known for the three towering pyramids and carved-stone sphinx that dominate the landscape, a vast complex of buildings and tombs lie hidden beneath centuries of wind-blown sand. It promised extraordinary treasures and insights into the workings of an ancient civilization at the pinnacle of its development.

Concessions or permits to excavate at Giza were granted in 1902 by Gaston Maspero, director of the Egyptian Antiquities Service. Maspero was intent on stopping the illicit looting and destruction of Egypt's most historic monuments and divided the plateau among Italian, German, and American missions. Ernesto Schiaparelli led the Italian team, Ludwig Borchardt (for Georg Steindorff) represented the Germans, and the Americans were headed by Reisner. The manner in which the competing parties were awarded the concessions is vividly recounted in Reisner's notes:

> In December, 1902, the three concessionaires met on the veranda of the Mena House Hotel. Everybody wanted a portion of the great Western Cemetery. It was divided in three strips East-West. Three bits of paper were marked 1, 2, and 3 and put in a hat. Mrs. Reisner drew the papers and presented one to each of us. The southern strip fell to the Italians,[1] the middle one to the Germans and the northern one to me. Then we proceeded to divide the pyramids. I perceived that the Italians were interested in the First Pyramid (Khufu's) and the Germans in the Second (Khafre's)...I was perfectly willing to have the Third Pyramid (Menkaure's)...[2]

Reisner's early field work in Egypt was under the auspices of the University of California, Berkeley, with funding for excavations at sites such as Naga ed-Deir, Ballas, and Giza provided by Phoebe Apperson Hearst, mother of newspaper mogul William Randolph Hearst. Born in the American Midwest in 1867, Reisner earned undergraduate

Painted limestone statue of Nefu and Khenetemsetju, Dynasty 5.

Fig. 17
George Andrew Reisner,
June 26, 1933.

and graduate degrees in Semitic languages and history at Harvard University. After gradu-
ation, he focused his energies on Egyptology, studying several years in Berlin with philolo-
gists Adolf Erman and Kurt Sethe. By 1896, Reisner was back in the U.S. and lecturing at
Harvard. He would soon embark upon a journey that would remain his lifelong pas-
sion—archaeological fieldwork. Along the way, he would become a pioneering force in
the application of scientific methodology to his profession.

Reisner began work on the tombs (mastabas) of officials who served under King
Khufu in Giza's great Western Cemetery (fig. 19).[3] The choicest were in close proximity to
the pyramid, providing a tangible symbol of a person's status in life, and by inference, in
the afterlife. The oldest of these tombs were arranged in a highly organized pattern of
streets and each consisted of two parts—a superstructure of brick or stone and a subterranean burial chamber (fig. 18). The superstructure was rectangular in shape with a stone
or rubble core, a flat top, and inward sloping walls that were sometimes faced with stone.
By the 4th Dynasty, small chapels had been added to the superstructure with rectangular
stelae featuring the deceased seated before a table of offerings (fig. 20). The stelae eventually evolved into elaborate false doors (cat. nos. 24, 44) that facilitated the passage of the
spirit, or *ka*, of the deceased from the burial chamber into the land of the living. Offerings
of either actual or model foods were often set on a table placed in front of the false door.

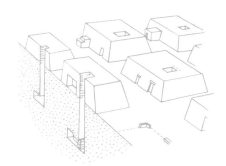

Fig. 18
Mastaba tomb construction.

Fig. 19
General view of the Western
Cemetery, looking west, from the
top of the Great Pyramid of
Khufu, June 25, 1932.

Also attached to the chapel was a sealed statue chamber, called a *serdab*, with sculptures of the owner. A small slit in the serdab's wall enabled the deceased to participate in ritual offerings provided by priests or visitors.

By Dynasty 5, mastaba chapels evolved into a series of rooms that were sometimes decorated with images and brief biographies of the deceased as well as representations and textual lists of goods for the afterlife. Some even included lively scenes of daily life such as harvesting, boating, and craft production. The largest and most extensively decorated chapels were built by Egypt's elite as signs of their status and power in this life and the next. In most mastabas, access to the burial chamber was located behind the false door and down a deep vertical shaft and a short horizontal passageway. This room, which contained the sarcophagus, was typically cut into the bedrock or lined with stone during Dynasty 4 and contained few, if any burial items. An exception to this rule are the "reserve heads" whose purpose is not completely understood (cat. nos. 9, 10; fig. 21).[4]

When Hearst support for his fieldwork came to an end in 1904,[5] Reisner was forced to look elsewhere for a sponsor.[6] By then, his reputation as a scholar and excavator was firmly established. Fortuitously, Harvard University and the Museum of Fine

Arts, Boston, were searching for someone to head a field expedition in Egypt. Their goals—to advance learning in scientific archaeology and to add works with unquestioned provenance to the Museum's growing collection—were met in what turned out to be a long and productive collaboration.

## MENKAURE'S PYRAMID COMPLEX

In 1906 Reisner began his work on the pyramid complex of Menkaure at the southernmost end of the great Giza diagonal (fig. 23). The smallest of the three main Giza pyramids, this monument abuts a dip on the plateau known as the Mokkatam Formation.[7] It includes the king's pyramid, an adjoining temple, and three satellite pyramids for his queens. A causeway connecting the pyramid temple to a smaller temple located in the valley was largely under sand. Named "Menkaure is Divine," the pyramid of the dynasty's fifth ruler was dressed in white Tura limestone except for its lower courses, which were encased in red granite. It measures 65 meters in height, is 102.2 meters by 104.6 meters at the base, and slopes at an angle of approximately 51 degrees.

Fig. 22

Line drawing of a cross section of a pyramid.

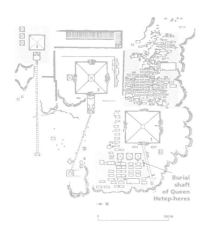

Fig. 23

Drawing: Map of the Giza necropolis, showing the pyramids and the Western and Eastern cemeteries.

Photo: Aerial view of the Giza plateau (Great Pyramid of Khufu in the foreground, with the pyramids of Khafre and Menkaure in the background), looking southwest, mid-20th century.

As with its immediate predecessors, the Menkaure pyramid employs an east-west axial orientation, aligning the sides of the monument in the true north position. This alignment was accomplished with astonishing accuracy, illustrating the importance of cardinality in Giza's cluster of pyramids. Mark Lehner suggests that the Egyptians determined true north by measuring the movement of the sun and its shadow and then plotted a perfect square on the ground that was subsequently leveled. A stone platform served as a foundation for blocks set in horizontal steps or tiers. Temporary ramps, composed of limestone chips, talfa, and gypsum, were constructed to expedite the transport of heavy stones upwards while casing blocks, dressed to produce a smooth, polished plane, were custom-fitted to the surface.[8]

It has been estimated that two crews of two thousand men each—mostly peasant conscripts—were needed to build the Great Pyramid. Thousands more, however, served in support roles as metalsmiths, potters, bakers, and brewers. The workforce for each of the Giza pyramids lived in tax-exempt towns established near the construction site. Their simple, mudbrick dwellings were largely abandoned after the pyramid was built. However, those involved in administering the cult of the king after his death continued to populate the plateau.

Access to Menkaure's burial chamber is on the pyramid's north side, about 4 meters above the base. A descending passage leads into a paneled chamber that exits into another passage with three portcullis blocks. These large granite stones, installed to prevent theft, block the entrance to a horizontal passage that opens into a large antechamber.[9] The room, hewn from bedrock and possibly an earlier burial chamber, is situated directly under the vertical axis of the pyramid. From here, a short passage slopes downward into the granite-lined burial chamber (fig. 22). The king's basalt sarcophagus, decorated with a carved, palace-façade motif, was removed in 1837 by Richard William Howard Vyse. An English army officer, Vyse reportedly used dynamite while exploring the pyramids.[10] To make matters worse, the sarcophagus was lost when the ship transporting it to England sank off the coast of Spain.

However, it was not Menkaure's pyramid but its associated temples that drew Reisner's attention. The pyramid temple (also called the mortuary temple) located along the pyramid's eastern side started out as a stone building but was finished in mudbrick after Menkaure's death by his successor, Shepseskaf. The structure included a processional ramp, vestibule, rectangular courtyard, colonnaded portico, sanctuary, and storehouses. Within the building and its immediate environs, the excavation team found fragments of a colossal statue of the seated king. This magnificent sculpture, carved in translucent

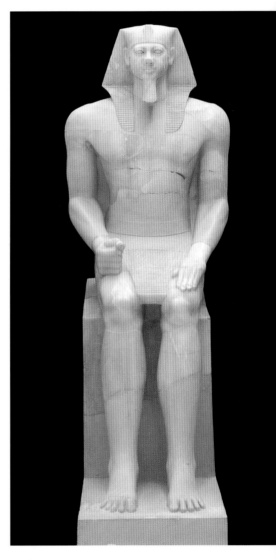

Fig. 24

Head from a colossal alabaster statue of King Menkaure *in situ*, April 14, 1907.

Colossal alabaster statue of King Menkaure.

alabaster, was probably the focal point in the courtyard (fig. 24). Fragments of other statues of Menkaure (cat. no. 7) were also recovered from this part of the complex.[11]

In 1908 Reisner and field director Oric Bates projected the axis of the temple
causeway and began the search for Menkaure's Valley Temple.[12] At the mouth of the
main wadi, they found the remains of a structure that had undergone three building
phases: a stone foundation laid by Menkaure, a mudbrick temple built by his son
Shepseskhaf, and a mudbrick restoration undertaken by Pepy II of Dynasty 6 after a
flood.[13] Excavating the southwest corner of the building, they discovered the now-
famous pair statue of King Menkaure and a queen (fig. 8) and a series of greywacke triads featuring King Menkaure, the goddess Hathor, and nome deities (cat. no. 5; fig. 25).
Although Reisner believed that there were several dozen triads, one for each nome, or
administrative province, a recent interpretation is that there were originally eight group
sculptures symbolizing major sites associated with the cult of Hathor.[14]

Over the next three decades, the Boston team divided their energies among twenty-
three sites in Egypt and Nubia (the Sudan). In fact, Reisner's discoveries in the land occupied by Egypt's southern neighbor were as extraordinary as his Giza finds. And, at each
site, he followed a meticulous program of record keeping, documenting each aspect of the
excavation with detailed maps, plans, notes, inventories, and photographs.[15] His goal

Fig. 29
Removing the stone sarcophagus
from the tomb of Queen
Hetepheres I, April 17, 1927.

Reisner's and an artist whose paintings of archaeological sites in Egypt form part of the Museum's documentary record, was present during the tension-filled event. He was later described as turning to Reisner and exclaiming in a loud voice, "George, she's a dud!" Reisner responded: "Gentlemen, I regret Queen Hetepheres is not receiving."[16]

The mystery of the unplundered tomb and empty sarcophagus of Hetepheres I led Reisner to conclude that the Expedition had discovered a reburial, the original interment having been in Dahshur near the pyramid of her husband Sneferu. He surmised that shortly after the queen's death, her tomb was entered and robbed. The thieves were probably caught in the act and the queen's son, Khufu, arranged a second burial near his own pyramid at Giza. As for the mummy, it was in all likelihood torn apart as the robbers hurriedly ripped jewels from the body. All that remained were embalming materials used during mummification stored within a canopic chest. Although Reisner's account has been challenged over the years, it continues to offer the most reasonable explanation for several strange facts such as the absence of a superstructure, the small, unfinished burial chamber, the presence of sherds from the same vessel in different areas of the tomb, and the chip in the sarcophagus's lid.[17]

## GIZA'S RULING ELITE

Between the years 1905 and 1941, the Expedition systematically excavated the Old
Kingdom tombs of Egypt's ruling class. In 1927, while clearing the mastabas of Khufu's
sons and daughters in the Eastern Cemetery, Reisner uncovered the three-room tomb
chapel of Queen Meresankh III—a granddaughter of Khufu, a daughter of Prince Kawab
(cat. no. 12) and Queen Hetepheres II, and the wife of Khafre (cat. nos. 3, 4). The rock-
cut chapel, believed to have been built by Hetepheres II for her daughter, was unusual in
that it was underground rather than part of the superstructure.[18] It also contained multiple, life-sized statues of both women carved out of the bedrock (fig. 30) and walls decorated with painted reliefs depicting Meresankh and her family, preparations for the afterlife, and outdoor scenes (fig. 31). Reisner recalled,

> Our eyes were first startled by the vivid colors of the reliefs and inscriptions around
> the northern part of this large chamber. None of us had ever seen anything like it.
> Then gradually, in the obscurity of the two adjoining rooms, statues and statuettes
> became visible…sixteen figures cut in the rock and four inserted in a niche in the
> south wall.[19]

Among the artifacts found in the burial are the first known set of canopic jars and a
unique pair statue of Hetepheres II and Meresankh III.[20] Hetepheres, shown standing to
the proper right of the younger queen, wears a heavy, shoulder-length wig and affection-

Fig. 30
Subterranean chamber in the
tomb of Queen Meresankh III,
May 8, 1927.

Fig. 31
Drawing of Queen Hetepheres II
and Queen Meresankh III in a boat
from the east wall, main room,
tomb of Meresankh III, Giza.

ately embraces her daughter with her left arm (fig. 32). Other distinctive aspects of the tomb are two inscriptions on the tomb's outer door—one stating the date of Meresankh's death, the other her funeral date.

The Boston team also continued to make exceptional finds in the Western Cemetery. Of particular interest is the late 5th Dynasty family burial of the overseer and purification-priest Akhmeretnesut (cat. no. 20). Reisner and assistant Clarence Fisher began excavating the tomb in 1912 but work on the mastaba, which had undergone several modifications and contained seven shafts, was not completed until 1935. Other mastabas such as the 5th Dynasty tomb of the pyramid-temple priest Penmeru yielded outstanding sculpture.[21] A triad featuring three representations of the deceased, as well as a family group with two figures of Penmeru, his wife Meretites, and two children (all located in the statue chamber of Penmeru's mastaba) are among the finest group statues known to exist (fig. 33).

One of the most interesting of the tomb complexes at Giza is the mastaba grouping of the Senedjemib family. Located near the northwest corner of Khufu's pyramid, it contains the burials of eight men who represent four generations of high officials, most of them architects and viziers. These men served a succession of late 5th and 6th Dynasty kings, and their tombs reflect a century of architectural, artistic, and economic change. The burial of the last member of the family interred at the site, Ptahshepses Impy (cat. nos. 38–41), was intact when discovered. Its form and contents offer insights into the twilight days of the Old Kingdom.

While other activities at Giza may have lacked the suspense and drama surrounding the discovery of

Hetepheres I's tomb, their scope and depth have added greatly to our understanding of the period. Reisner had many assistants and colleagues in Egypt and Boston, and their efforts, both scholarly and curatorial, greatly benefited the Museum and the growing field of Egyptology. In particular, Dows Dunham, William Stevenson Smith, and William Kelly Simpson left a rich and enduring legacy. The Museum continues to explore the Giza plateau and its ongoing publication, the *Giza Mastaba Series*, serves as a model of archaeological documentation.[22]

Fig. 33

Limestone group statue of Penmeru, Dynasty 5.

## NOTES

1. Boston was assigned the Italian concession in 1905. For results of the Italian expedition see Curto 1963.

2. Although it was the smallest of the three Giza pyramids (one-tenth of the building mass of Khufu's pyramid), Reisner's assistant Arthur Mace had already determined on a scouting mission that Menkaure's pyramid promised rich finds. See Lehner 1997, 134. For the quote, see Reisner n.d. a, 5.

3. The Eastern Cemetery contained the tombs of Khufu's wives and close relatives.

4. The "reserve heads" that date to the reigns of Khufu and Khafre were found in either the tomb shaft or burial chamber. See Roehrig 1999e, 73–75.

5. Reisner states that Mrs. Hearst experienced a financial setback in South Dakota's Homestake mine. Reisner n.d. a, 6.

6. Dunham 1958, 21.

7. Lehner 1997, 106.

8. Lehner 1997, 212–17.

9. It appears that all attempts to secure access to burials were circumvented by ingenious robbers. See Arnold 1991, 222–24.

10. Lehner 1997, 50–53.

11. Reisner 1931, 108, pls.12–17.

12. Reisner 1931, 34–35.

13. Reisner 1911, 17–20.

14. Wood 1974, 82–93.

15. The Expedition's records are divided into daily dairies, photographs, and object registers. For a detailed description of the documents, see Dunham 1958, 23–24.

16. Smith 1956, 148.

17. Mark Lehner believes this to have been the queen's original tomb, the body having been removed after layout changes were made in the Eastern Cemetery; see Lehner 1985. More recently, Hans-Hubertus Münch interprets the find as the queen's funerary deposit rather than as a reburial; see Münch 2000, 898–908.

18. For a detailed discussion of the tomb (G 7540), see Reisner 1927b, 64–79 and Dunham and Simpson 1974.

19. Reisner 1927b, 64.

20. For a discussion of the statue, now in the collection of the Museum of Fine Arts, Boston (MFA 30.1456), see Capel 1996, 103–4.

21. Porter and Moss 1974, 82–83. See also Smith 1946, 53, pl. 21b, c.

22. The series has just published its seventh volume and several additional manuscripts are in progress.

# Dynasty 4

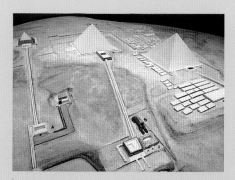

Fig. 34
Model of the Giza plateau
(scale 1:2000), 1998.

Fig. 35
Seated limestone statues of Prince
Rahotep and Nofret, from Meidum,
Dynasty 4, reign of Sneferu.

Although the massive stone blocks, life-sized statues, and enclosure walls of King Djoser's Step Pyramid complex of Dynasty 3 provided a template for future royal burials, 4th Dynasty rulers refined and altered the plan. The north-south layout became an east-west orientation while the stepped superstructure evolved into the true pyramid form. The pyramid temple originally located on the northern face moved to the center of the eastern base, and a causeway leading to another temple in the valley was added (fig 34). Some of these architectural developments reflect ideological changes concerning kingship and the growing influence of the powerful sun cult at Heliopolis. In this context, the true pyramid represents an expanding ray of light illuminating the earth from above. This interpretation is in keeping with spell 523 from the Pyramid Texts. It suggests that the dead king ascends heavenward to unite with the god Re via the sun's rays, thereby becoming part of an eternal cycle of renewal.[1] The addition of Re to the king's titulary, beginning with King Redjedef (2560–2555 B.C.), formally established the association. Another viewpoint places the pyramid at the state's political center and identifies the pyramid's monumentality and location in the necropolis as concrete expressions of the tight central organization that characterized the period.[2]

Private tombs also reflected the political dynamics of the dynasty. Proximity to the pyramid was reserved for those of rank whose welfare—in this life and the next—depended upon the largesse of the king. Members of the royal family often held the highest posts, including that of chief executive officer or vizier. A case in point is Hemiunu (cat. no. 13), vizier under Khufu (2585–2560 B.C.) and owner of one of the largest mastabas in the Western Cemetery. As for private tomb substructures, there is a shift away from multiroom arrangements that resemble houses to single chambers with few grave goods. Accompanying these changes were new attitudes toward the hereafter based on the belief that the king would sustain the deceased in perpetuity.[3]

The human and material resources needed to complete the building projects of 4th Dynasty kings reflect a period of social and economic stability. In fact, Egypt's rulers were so powerful that they extended their influence far beyond their own borders. The founder of the dynasty, Sneferu (2625–2585 B.C.), is known to have sent troops into Nubia to secure Egypt's southern border and protect the quarries, gold mines, and trade routes for luxury goods such as panther skins and ostrich eggs. In another campaign during his reign against Libya, both prisoners and cattle were obtained while an Egyptian presence in the Sinai guaranteed continued exploitation of the region's copper mines. To meet the demand for building materials such as cedar, fleets of commercial ships sailed to destinations in Lebanon and Syria.[4] Later kings, notably Khufu and Khafre (2555–2532 B.C.), followed a similar foreign policy.

The builders of the pyramid complexes numbered in the thousands.[5] They included quarrymen, stone haulers, masons, metal workers, and artisans. Many were peasant conscripts organized into crews of one thousand men divided into five groups, or *phyles*. They lived in settlements on the plateau and were provided with daily rations of bread, beer, and fish. Priests and officials who maintained the cult of the king also lived in the necropolis. They occupied tax-exempt districts and tended to the produce and livestock supplied by provincial estates.

The royal workshops, located in precincts around the pyramid, were part of industrial compounds that employed skilled workers.[6] Among these workers were potters, metalworkers, and sculptors. The statuary created during this dynamic, innovative period includes some of the finest works ever to be produced (fig. 35). Idealized, elegant, and restrained—they established a canon of body proportions that endured throughout the course of Egyptian history. YJM

1. Edwards 1985, 299–301.

2. O'Connor 1984, 19–21.

3. Roth 1993, 49–50, stresses the dependence of officials on the generosity of the king, pointing out the decreased distance between royal and private tombs at Giza.

4. Grimal 1992, 67–71.

5. Lehner 1997, 224–25, estimates that twenty to twenty-five thousand workers built the Khufu pyramid.

6. Lehner 1997, 238–39.

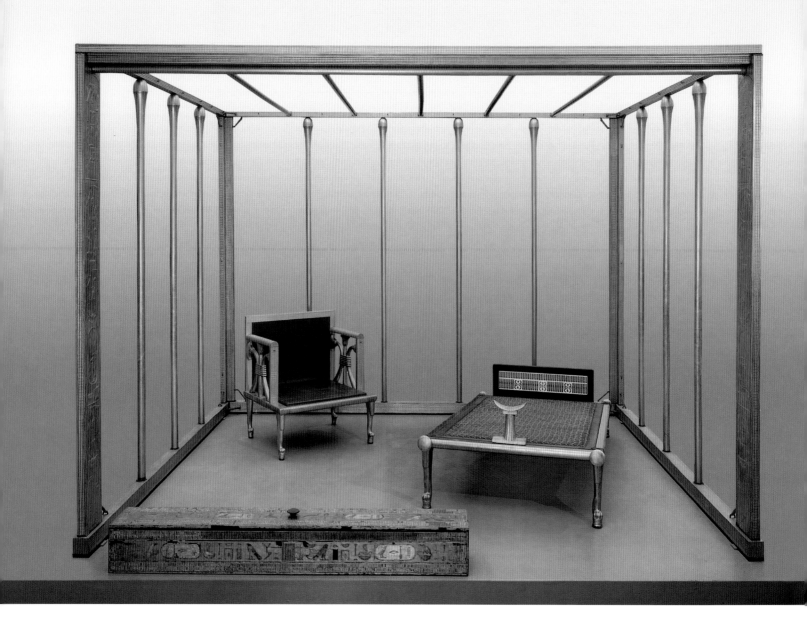

The entrance to Queen Hetepheres I's tomb, 1925 or 1926.

**1 | FURNITURE AND INLAYS FROM THE TOMB OF QUEEN HETEPHERES I**

a. Bed canopy (Reproduction by Joseph Gerte)
Dynasty 4, reign of Sneferu, 2625–2585 B.C.
Giza, tomb G 7000 X
Wood, gold sheet
L. 313.7 cm, h. 221.5 cm, w. 258.8 cm
Departmental Appropriation 38.873

The Giza tomb of Queen Hetepheres I, most likely the wife of Sneferu and mother of Khufu, contained the remains of a unique collection of furniture excavated by George Reisner and Dows Dunham in 1925 and 1926.[1] During the 326 days it took to clear the queen's tomb, each step was meticulously recorded and documented. The burial chamber presented a special challenge, as the wooden component of the queen's funerary equipment had largely collapsed and disintegrated, leaving an ash-like residue among the scattered gold encasements and inlays (fig. 28, p. 41).

Reisner's methods proved invaluable when attempts were later made to reconstruct the extraordinary furniture suite found in the burial.[2] The suite included a square canopy, a curtain box, a bed with headrest, two armchairs, a carrying chair, and a jewelry casket.[3] Although the wood had largely deteriorated, the gold and copper sheathing covering the wooden surfaces survived.[4] Reisner described the metalwork as extremely fine; and on several items, including the carrying chair and jewel box, the queen is identified by name and title.[5]

The recreated bed canopy is composed of a gold-encased wooden frame with three floor beams, four upright posts at the corners,[6] ten slender columns, four roof beams, and five roofing poles. The copper-covered joints are bound by leather strips secured to copper staples.[7] A series of copper hooks along the floor and roof beams would have served as fasteners for the linen curtain panels.[8] These panels were probably stored in the long, rectangular box bearing the names, titles, and images of Sneferu, the queen's husband.[9] Another box, a replica of an inscribed jewel casket, now houses Hetepheres's silver bangles. Inlaid with semi-precious stones arranged in a repeat butterfly pattern, these adornments are representative of the "stacked bracelet" style popular among court ladies during the late 3rd, 4th, and 5th Dynasties.[10]

A central component of the suite is the sloped, rectangular bed with a leather-webbed frame in the center, a footboard decorated with faience, and four leonine legs. A wooden headrest sheathed in gold and silver sheet completes the sleeping unit. The low, wide armchair incorporates rope-bound papyrus stalks in the sides and repeats the lion-leg motif found on the bed. The construction and inscription on the carrying chair suggest that it is later in date, possibly a gift from the queen's son Khufu. The gold hieroglyphs on the back were originally set into strips of ebony, while the ends of the carrying poles feature palm leaf capitals covered by heavy gold sheet. YJM

1. For a discussion of the queen's name and titles, see Baud 1999, 2:525–27.

2. The excavators created more than one thousand photographs and nearly two thousand pages of notes and drawings. For an overview of the project, see Reisner 1927a, 13–36, and Reisner and Smith 1955, 13–47. W. A. Stewart and Bernard Rice accomplished the actual work on the Cairo canopy. Stewart fabricated the bed, headrest, carrying chair, and jewel box. In Egypt, materials expert Alfred Lucas and Egyptian conservator Ahmed Youssef aided Stewart and Rice. The Boston suite, excluding the curtain box, was fabricated by Boston cabinetmaker Joseph Gerte several years after the Cairo grouping was reconstructed.

3. Many other wooden boxes (much deteriorated by the time the tomb was opened) contained pottery, textiles, and other equipment for the afterlife.

4. Both on and near the gold casings associated with the bed and curtain box were faience inlays. These were later incorporated into the Cairo suite.

5. The hieroglyphs on the canopy jambs are raised relief worked from the underside (*repoussé*) with chased detailing on the front. Some signs, such as the bee in *nisut bity* (part of the king's titulary), are exceptional in that they demonstrate an attempt at foreshortening.

6. The interior panels of the two posts served as entrance jambs where an inscription gives the names and titles of Hetepheres's husband, King Sneferu.

7. The joints between the roof beams, jambs, and floor rails are mortise-and-tenon joints; the roofing poles are connected to the roof beams by dovetail joints.

8. For a detailed discussion of the reconstruction, see Reisner 1932a.

9. The inscriptions appear on the lid and sides, while the images of Sneferu are on the ends. Both the hieroglyphs and the images were enhanced by brightly colored faience inlays set into the wood.

10. For a discussion of the dating, usage, and construction of these ornaments, see Markowitz, Haynes, and Lacovara 2002.

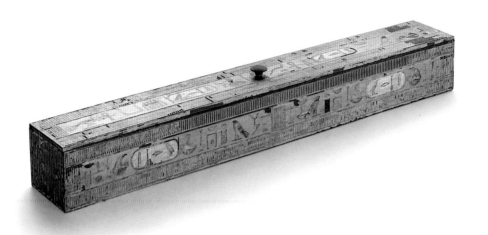

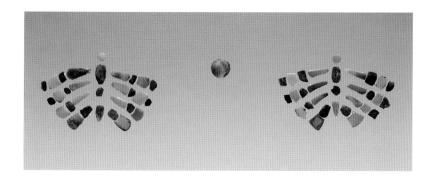

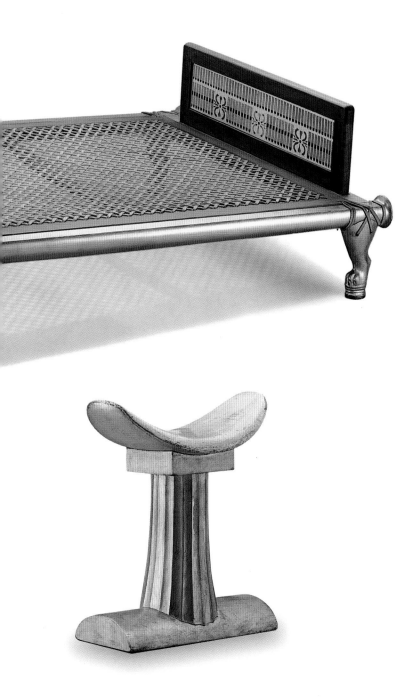

b. Curtain box (Reproduction by Ahmed Youssef)
Dynasty 4, reign of Sneferu, 2625–2585 B.C.
Giza, tomb G 7000 X
Wood, gold sheet, silver, faience
L. 157.5 cm, h. 18.5 cm, w. 21.5 cm
Harvard University-Museum of Fine Arts
Expedition 39.746

c. Butterfly inlays from a silver bracelet
Dynasty 4, reign of Sneferu to Khufu,
2625–2560 B.C.
Giza, tomb G 7000 X
Lapis lazuli, turquoise, carnelian
L. 15.5 cm, h. 0.3 cm, w. 7 cm (including mount)
Harvard University-Museum of Fine Arts
Expedition 47.1701

d. Armchair (Reproduction by Joseph Gerte)
Dynasty 4, reign of Sneferu to Khufu,
2625–2560 B.C.
Giza, tomb G 7000 X
Wood, gold sheet
H. 79.5 cm, w. 70.7 cm, d. 66 cm
Gift of Mrs. Charles Gaston Smith and Group of Friends 38.957

e. Bed (Reproduction by Joseph Gerte)
Dynasty 4, reign of Sneferu to Khufu,
2625–2560 B.C.
Giza, tomb G 7000 X
Wood, gold sheet, leather
L. 177 cm, h. 43.5 cm, w. 97.5 cm
Harvard University-Museum of Fine Arts
Expedition 29.1858

f. Carrying chair (Reproduction by Joseph Gerte)
Dynasty 4, reign of Khufu, 2585–2560 B.C.
Giza, tomb G 7000 X
Cypress, ebony, gilt copper, gold-plated electrotypes
H. 79.5 cm, w. 70.7 cm, d. 66 cm
Gift of Mrs. Charles Gaston Smith and Group of Friends 38.874

g. Headrest (Reproduction by Joseph Gerte)
Dynasty 4, reign of Sneferu to Khufu,
2625–2560 B.C.
Giza, tomb G 7000 X
Wood, gold, silver sheet
H. 20.5 cm, w. 17.2 cm, d. 7.8 cm
Harvard University-Museum of Fine Arts
Expedition 29.1859

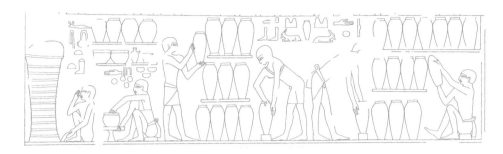

Craftsmen in the pottery workshop of
Ti at Saqqara, Dynasty 6

## 2 CERAMICS FROM THE TOMB OF QUEEN HETEPHERES I

a. Jar
Dynasty 4, reign of Sneferu to Khufu,
2625–2560 B.C.
Giza, tomb G 7000 X
Nile silt
H. 22.9 cm, diam. 19.2 cm
Harvard University-Museum of Fine Arts
Expedition 37.2696

b. Bowl with flaring rim
Dynasty 4, reign of Sneferu to Khufu,
2625–2560 B.C.
Giza, tomb G 7000 X
Nile silt
H. 8.6 cm, diam. 22 cm
Harvard University-Museum of Fine Arts
Expedition 37.2698

c. Footed vessel
Dynasty 4, reign of Sneferu to Khufu,
2625–2560 B.C.
Giza, tomb G 7000 X
Nile silt
H. 24.5 cm, diam. 34 cm
Harvard University-Museum of Fine Arts
Expedition 37.2691

d. Bowl
Dynasty 4, reign of Sneferu to Khufu,
2625–2560 B.C.
Giza, tomb G 7000 X
Nile silt
H. 4.7 cm, diam. 19.7 cm
Harvard University-Museum of Fine Arts
Expedition 37.2695

e. Spouted bowl with recurved rim
Dynasty 4, reign of Sneferu to Khufu,
2625–2560 B.C.
Giza, tomb G 7000 X
Nile silt
H. 19.2 cm, diam. 34.2 cm
Harvard University-Museum of Fine Arts
Expedition 37.2688

f. Jar stand
Dynasty 4, reign of Sneferu to Khufu,
2625–2560 B.C.
Giza, tomb G 7000 X
Nile silt
H. 11.1 cm, diam. 10.8 cm
Harvard University-Museum of Fine Arts
Expedition 37.2736

g. Small jar
Dynasty 4, reign of Sneferu to Khufu,
2625–2560 B.C.
Giza, tomb G 7000 X
Nile silt
H. 6.8 cm, diam. 6.6 cm
Harvard University-Museum of Fine Arts
Expedition 37.2668

h. Lid
Dynasty 4, reign of Sneferu to Khufu,
2625–2560 B.C.
Giza, tomb G 7000 X
Nile silt
H. 7.5 cm, diam. 18 cm
Harvard University-Museum of Fine Arts
Expedition 37.2712

i. Model bowl
Dynasty 4, reign of Sneferu to Khufu,
2625–2560 B.C.
Giza, tomb G 7000 X
Nile silt
H. 2.8 cm, diam. 8.6 cm
Harvard University-Museum of Fine Arts
Expedition 37.2666

j. Bag-shaped vessel
Dynasty 4, reign of Sneferu to Khufu,
2625–2560 B.C.
Giza, tomb G 7000 X
Nile silt
H. 11.2 cm, diam. 13.5 cm
Harvard University-Museum of Fine Arts
Expedition 37.2649

The Egyptians used Nile silt and marl clays for pottery destined for the household, temple, and tomb. The silt, rich in organic matter, silica, and iron oxides, was particularly abundant and readily available. Dynasty 4 potters shaped their clay by hand or by turning it on a wheel.[1] Completed vessels were then heated, turning them reddish brown, and sometimes the porous surfaces were coated with a wash or slip.[2] Further enhancements included burnishing with a tool and polishing with a cloth.

The pottery from the tomb of Queen Hetepheres is an important, large corpus of vessels from a dated context. Although most of the vessels were found in fragments, George Reisner was able to devise a typology of shapes used during the reigns of Kings Sneferu and Khufu.[3] Many of the forms derive from older stone vessels or from containers made of metal.[4] Nearly all were fabricated from red-brown clay that was smoothed with a wet hand before drying. While surfaces were left undecorated, several forms, such as the bowl with flaring rim, received a red slip and high polish. YJM

1. Turning is much slower than throwing on a wheel. Throwing does not appear to have been used until Dynasty 5, as evidenced in a potter's scene in the tomb of Ti at Saqqara (line drawing at left). See Arnold and Bourriau 1993, 43.

2. Washes are composed of pigment and water while slip contains fine clay, pigment, and water.

3. Reisner concluded that many vessels were broken during the plundering of the Queen's original burial and that the pottery fragments were included in her reburial at Giza. Since the pottery was stored in wooden boxes, additional breakage occurred as the wood deteriorated and pots fell to the floor. In the end, Reisner was able to reconstruct 281 vessels. See Reisner and Smith 1955, 60–68, figs. 58–79. Reisner's typology for the period, though not complete, includes seventeen types and thirty-four sub-types.

4. The bag-shaped vessels, bowls with recurved rims, and neckless jars with plastic rims have metal precursors, while the flat-bottomed bowl with wide mouth and no rim appeared first in hard stone.

## 3 | HEAD OF KING KHAFRE

Dynasty 4, 2555–2532 B.C.
Giza, surface debris south of tomb G 2370
Egyptian alabaster
H. 19.3 cm, W. 17 cm, D. 16 cm
Harvard University-Museum of Fine Arts
Expedition 34.52a–b

The pyramid temples of Khafre, son of Khufu, were once adorned with countless statues in fine hard stone.[1] George Reisner found a few complete sculptures but recovered mostly fragments, including numerous pieces of Khafre statues in the surface debris around mastaba G 2370.[2] Reisner believed that sometime in the late Old Kingdom, when the royal sculptures were only fifty to one hundred years old, they were broken apart to make the ubiquitous and valued stone offering vessels.[3]

Such was likely the fate of this fragmentary head of Khafre that once belonged to a nearly life-sized sculpture of polished translucent alabaster. It wears a striated *nemes* with a narrow headband and a false beard.[4] Although much is missing, Khafre's recognizable facial features are still visible. Characteristic are the high, angular cheekbones that swell beneath the eye and again under the tail of the cosmetic eye line, and the use of elongated, squared-off raised ribbons for the cosmetic eye line and eyebrow. The broad mouth with its upper and lower lips of nearly equal thickness is also typical.[5] The refined features and subtle modeling indicate that this image of Khafre was certainly a masterpiece in its entirety. JLH

1. Ziegler 1999c, 252, identifies alabaster, black granite, quartzite, anorthosite gneiss, and schist or greywacke. Reisner 1931, 126, estimates between one and two hundred sculptures.

2. Smith 1946, 33–34; Ziegler 1999c, 252.

3. Reisner n.d. b, chapter IX, 20.

4. The raised band is only visible above the right ear. The back of the head is plain, as is the root of the tail of the headdress.

5. The corners of the mouth are softly drilled, and the centers of the upper and lower lips protrude. The philtrum is broken. The lower lip is not deeply undercut like that found on sculptures of Menkaure. See other Khafre sculptures with similar features in Smith 1946, pls. 12a–e; Metropolitan Museum 1999, nos. 56, 58–59, 61.

## 4 | HEAD OF KING KHAFRE

Dynasty 4, reign of Khafre, 2555–2532 B.C.
Giza, debris at the northeast corner of tomb G 5330
Egyptian alabaster
H. 20.4 cm, w. 12.5 cm, d. 10 cm
Harvard University-Museum of Fine Arts Expedition 21.351

This life-sized head is identified as King Khafre because it was found with a piece of statuary containing the king's *cartouche*,[1] and because of its resemblance to other extant Khafre images. The fine-grained, translucent white alabaster is also typical.[2] Many fragments of such statuary that once adorned Khafre's pyramid temples have been excavated from various locations in Giza's Western Cemetery. George Reisner believed that they were dragged to these places and broken up for the manufacture of stone offering vessels.[3]

This fragmentary head was reconstructed from four pieces, two large and two small. It is adorned with a *uraeus* and has a slightly raised headband, all that remains of the now missing *nemes*. Overall, the face is youthful with smooth cheeks and minimal subtle modeling. It is an idealized image, and the pronounced "v" dip in the upper lip between the philtrum lines is a feature common to many Khafre sculptures. The fluidly curving, raised-relief eyebrows are distinctive, as they are closer together than their counterparts on other images of the king. The fleshy, rounded nose reveals the family resemblance to Khafre's son, King Menkaure.[4]

JLH

1. Reisner 1931, 128, no. 4.
2. Ziegler 1999c, 252.
3. Smith 1946, 33; Reisner 1931, 128, no. 4.
4. Smith 1946, pl.12c–e.

## 5 KING MENKAURE, THE GODDESS HATHOR, AND THE DEIFIED HARE NOME

Dynasty 4, reign of Menkaure, 2532–2510 B.C.
Giza, Menkaure Valley Temple
Greywacke
H. 84.5 cm, w. 43.5 cm, d. 49 cm
Harvard University-Museum of Fine Arts Expedition  09.200

George Reisner discovered some of the finest Egyptian sculpture known to exist in the Menkaure Valley Temple.[1] An extraordinary pair statue of King Menkaure and a queen was unearthed there (fig. 8, p. 25), as well as a series of triads, each depicting the king, the goddess Hathor, and a personified nome god.[2] The context and precise meaning of the triads is not well understood. According to an early theory, there were originally thirty or more, one for each of the thirty-odd nomes. Their presence in the pyramid complex guaranteed the deceased king a continuous supply of provisions from all regions of the country.[3] A more recent interpretation is that there were eight sculptures, symbolizing the major sites associated with the cult of Hathor.[4]

The sensitively modeled and beautifully proportioned triad illustrated here is unique in that Hathor, rather than Menkaure, dominates the group by her central and forward position and larger scale. A major deity since Predynastic times, Hathor was the celestial mother of the sun calf, a guardian of the necropolis, and the protectress of the king. Depicted with gentle curves in contrast to the block seat and the rectangular slab in the back, Hathor's left arm embraces Menkaure's waist while her right crosses her midsection to rest on the king's arm.[5] The goddess' face is full and round, with subtle modeling of the eyebrows, folds on the upper eyelids,[6] a small mouth with puckered lips, and a chin that recedes slightly. Her headdress, a solar disc and cow horns,[7] is prominently displayed above an incised, tripartite wig, but the jewelry that once adorned her sleeveless sheath dress—a *wesekh* broadcollar with teardrop pendants and a wide band bracelet—have largely disappeared.[8]

Menkaure stands on Hathor's left with his left foot advanced. His remarkably individualized facial features—the prominent eyes, fleshy nose, moustache,[9] and protruding lower lip—are all characteristics recognizable on other representations of the king. Unlike the female figures in the group, Menkaure's musculature is well defined, giving the overall impression of a youthful, athletic, and forceful ruler. His arms are at his sides with the left hand holding a ritual cloth or staff while the right clasps a hafted, ceremonial mace.[10] He wears the white crown of Upper Egypt, a false beard,[11] and a pleated *shendyt* kilt with belt. A painted neck ornament in the form of a multistrand, beaded collar and a pair of bracelets once completed his attire.[12]

Standing to Hathor's right is a personification of the Hermopolite or Hare nome. Each of ancient Egypt's nomes or provinces was associated with a male or female deity.[13] This nome deity wears the Hare standard (a symbol of her district) on her head, and holds an *ankh* in her left hand. Carved into the base is an inscription that reads: "The Horus Kakhet, King of Upper and Lower Egypt, Menkaure, beloved of Hathor, Mistress of the Sycamore. Recitation—'I have given you all good things, all offerings, and all provisions in Upper Egypt, forever.'" YJM

1. Reisner 1931, 34–54, 108–115.

2. All together, four complete triads (MFA Boston 09.200, Cairo JE 46499, JE 40678, and JE 40679), one incomplete triad (MFA Boston 11.3147), and fragments from a sixth grouping were recovered from the site. See Reisner 1931, 110, no. 14. For the Cairo triads, see Pirelli 1999, 70–71.

3. Smith 1960, 46.

4. Wood 1974, 82–93.

5. This pose is the same (in reverse) as that of the queen in the pair statue from the same site (fig. 8).

6. Field photography shows black pigment on the eyebrows and around the eyes. The cosmetic lines extend outward, stopping at the end of the brow.

7. This headdress was not in standard use until Dynasty 5. However, the solar disk, a symbol of the sun god Re, indicates the increased importance of this deity by the end of Dynasty 4.

8. The ornaments are clearly visible in photographs taken in the field.

9. Traces of black pigment are still visible.

10. A mace, like the crook and flail, are symbols of earthly power.

11. A symbol of kingship. The beard's strap, originally painted black, is no longer visible.

12. Evident in field photography.

13. The Hermopolite nome was the fifteenth nome in Upper Egypt.

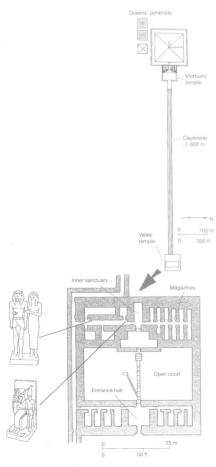

King Menkaure's pyramid complex.

## 6 | HEAD OF KING MENKAURE

Dynasty 4, reign of Menkaure, 2532–2510 B.C.
Giza, Menkaure Valley Temple
Egyptian alabaster
H. 29.2 cm, w. 19.6 cm, d. 21.9 cm
Harvard University-Museum of Fine Arts
Expedition 09.203

This alabaster head was once part of a seated, life-sized statue, one of four of Menkaure found in fragments by George Reisner in the king's valley temple.[1] The youthful quality of the face caused Reisner to propose that this was the head of Prince Shepseskaf, Menkaure's son.[2] However, this is undoubtedly Menkaure, as it shares many features with his other known representations: the blunt, rounded nose, full cheeks, bulging upper eye, prominent brow ridge, and deep undercut below the lower lip.

The head is adorned with a *uraeus*[3] and is covered with irregular and roughly carved horizontal grooves that represent either natural hair or, more likely, a tight-fitting wig or cap.[4] An unusual area behind the ears and at the back of the head is smooth. One explanation for this smooth area is that the king's headdress may have been recarved.[5] Because the area resembles the shape of wings wrapping around the king's head, another theory is that a falcon originally sat on the king's shoulder.[6] JLH

1. Reisner 1931, 36, 109–24, pls. 47–53. One of the four seated sculptures has been reconstructed and is now in the Cairo Museum; see pl. 48.

2. Reisner 1931, 114.

3. According to Johnson 1990, 108–9, this is the earliest representation of a *uraeus* lying directly on a horizontally striated head covering. Earlier examples of *uraei* are depicted with *nemes*. She notes that, amazingly, this is the only *uraeus* remaining intact from the Old Kingdom.

4. Each sideburn on Menkaure's head is different; the left has vertical striations and the right one is plain.

5. Peter Lacovara 1995b, 126, has suggested that an original *nemes* was cut away.

6. Roehrig 1999a, 276, note 6. See Verner 1985, 267–80, pls. 45–46; and Smith 1946, pl. Vc.

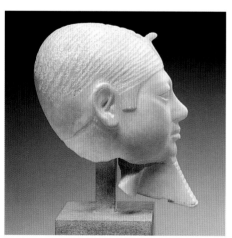

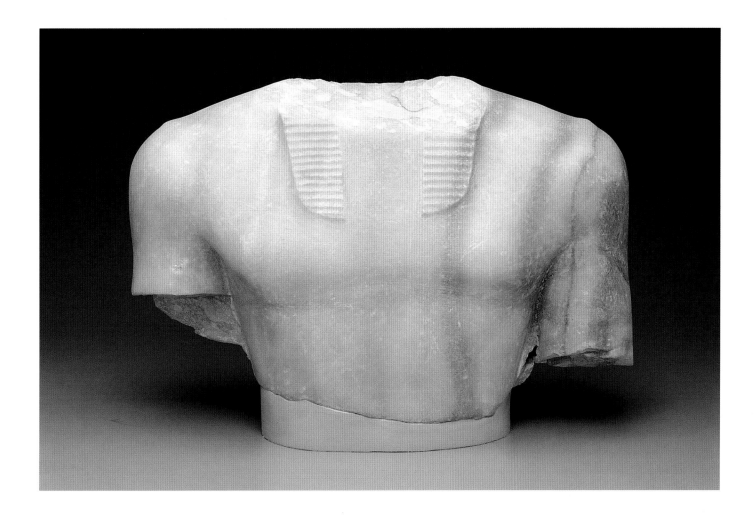

## 7 | TORSO OF KING MENKAURE

Dynasty 4, reign of Menkaure, 2532–2510
B.C.
Giza, Pyramid Temple of Menkaure
Egyptian alabaster
H. 31.8 cm, w. 46.4 cm, d. 19.7 cm
Harvard University-Museum of Fine Arts
Expedition 11.3146

The temple adjoining Menkaure's pyramid was
the largest of its type on the Giza plateau, perhaps reflecting an increased emphasis on the role
of the king as a direct descendant of the sun
god.[1] It consisted of an entrance hall, a large
court with limestone pavement and paneled
brick walls, a portico with double colonnade,
and an inner sanctuary of Tura limestone
flanked by numerous rooms and corridors.[2]

Outside the temple, about twelve feet from a
drain hole in a wall, excavators found fragments
of statuary depicting Menkaure (see photo at
left). Several fragments were joined to form this
life-size calcite torso.[3] The broad shoulders and
muscular outlines of the upper arms and chest
convey a youthful strength and vigor. Even the
back musculature, further defined by a subtle
vertical depression along the spine, supports the
impression of a physically ideal ruler. Remnants
of the *nemes* are visible on both the chest and

back. In the front are the pleated lappets, while
the ringed tail rests at mid-shoulder on the back.
YJM

1. Reisner 1931, 135.

2. For an account of the pyramid temple's excavation, see Reisner 1931, 9–33. Stadelmann 1997,
1–16, suggests that the pyramid temples at Giza
included false doors through which the deceased
king passed to partake of daily offerings.

3. The most important find at this site was an impos-
ing head from an alabaster colossus of the king. It
was later reunited with other fragments found in and
around the temple to form what is now object number 09.204 in the Museum of Fine Arts, Boston,
collection (see fig. 24, p. 37). In all likelihood, this
grand statue was once prominently displayed at the
end of a long corridor of red granite on the main
axis. For a list of the pyramid temple finds, see
Reisner 1931, 108.

## UNFINISHED STATUES OF KING MENKAURE

a. Unfinished statue of King Menkaure
Dynasty 4, reign of Menkaure, 2532–2510 B.C.
Giza, Menkaure Valley Temple
Anorthosite gneiss
H. 35 cm, w. 15.5 cm, d. 19.5 cm
Harvard University-Museum of Fine Arts
Expedition 11.731

b. Unfinished statue of King Menkaure
Dynasty 4, reign of Menkaure, 2532–2510 B.C.
Giza, Menkaure Valley Temple
Anorthosite gneiss
H. 43 cm, w. 16 cm, d. 24.7 cm
Harvard University-Museum of Fine Arts
Expedition 11.729

c. Unfinished statue of King Menkaure
Dynasty 4, reign of Menkaure, 2532–2510 B.C.
Giza, Menkaure Valley Temple
Anorthosite gneiss
H. 36 cm, w. 16 cm, d. 23.2 cm
Harvard University-Museum of Fine Arts
Expedition 11.732

While excavating the Menkaure Valley Temple, the Harvard-Boston team discovered fifteen statuettes in various states of completion.[1] Each statuette features the king seated on a throne, with arms bent at the elbows and feet flat on the base. In the more detailed examples, the king wears a *nemes* with a *uraeus*, a *shendyt*, and false beard. In addition, the left hand is presented open, palm down, on the left thigh, while the right hand is closed and resting on the right thigh.

The unfinished figures provide a visual record of the work habits of the ancient sculptor. George Reisner used the group to identify eight different steps of production. The earlier states represented by catalogue numbers 8a and 8b retain the red lines drawn by the artist on the quadrangular block. These contour lines, made to guide apprentice cutters, provided a silhouette of the desired form.[2] Once they were obliterated, new ones indicating areas in need of deeper carving were added, as on catalogue number 8c. In the final stages, finishing points were given to the emerging figure, the stone was polished with abrasives, and hieroglyphs identifying the person represented were carved into the base or back support. In all likelihood, the most skilled sculptors executed the final steps.[3]  YJM

1. Reisner 1931, 108–29.
2. There is no evidence for the use of squared grids during the Old Kingdom. See Robins 1994, 64.
3. Smith 1946, 105–12.

## 9 | RESERVE HEAD

Dynasty 4, probably reign of Khufu,
2585–2560 B.C.
Giza, tomb G 4140 A
Limestone
H. 27.3 cm, W. 17.5 cm, D. 25 cm
Harvard University-Museum of Fine Arts
Expedition 14.717

George Reisner coined the term "reserve head" according to his theory that such a head was an extra, or reserve, for the mummy. Few (between thirty-two and thirty-seven) are known, and their purpose and function have never been fully understood.[1] Their inclusion in burials appears to have been part of a short-lived practice that had no direct precedent and that did not evolve into another sculptural type.

The reserve heads are exceptional in many ways. For instance, it is highly unusual to find a sculpture of only a head in Egyptian art; most human representations are complete figures.[2] Also, aside from slab stelae, no other sculpted images have been found in tombs containing a reserve head. Further, while most sculptures have been found in either the offering chapel or serdab, reserve heads appear to have been placed in the burial chamber near the coffin.[3] The typically long, flat-bottomed necks indicate that they were meant to stand.[4] Most inexplicable is the seemingly intentional mutilation done to many of the reserve heads before burial. The damaging marks consist of roughly chiseled, deep grooves up the back of the head and around the hairline, as well as the destruction of noses and ears.[5] Even more puzzling is the ancient patching of the broken ears on certain examples. At present, there is no scholarly theory regarding their creation that can be supported by all extant reserve heads.[6]

This reserve head was the second found by George Reisner in mastaba G 4140. The other is credited to Meretites, the owner of the slab stela from the same tomb.[7] Reisner proposed that this more masculine face must represent Meretites's husband, but no inscriptional evidence supports his theory. Like all known reserve heads, the naturalistic features appear to represent a specific individual. This head has full cheeks, high cheekbones, deeply set eyes, and a prominent nose. The eyes are carved with great precision—a double line details the upper eye and lid and a beveled line defines the lower. The extended,

pointed inner canthus lines are typical of early 4th Dynasty sculpture. The eyebrows are defined only by an incised line at the bottom of the brow, much the same as the hairline across the forehead. The extraordinary craftsmanship reflects the work of a royal atelier. JLH

1. Reserve heads have been found for the most part in Old Kingdom mastaba tombs, primarily at Giza. Lacovara 1997, 28, attests thirty-two; Hawass 1995b, 97, says thirty-seven. According to Roehrig 1999e, 73, 79, twenty-seven were found at Giza and four were found outside Giza, one each from Lisht, Dashur, Sakkara, and Abusir.

2. The bust of Nefertity in Berlin and the bust of Ankhhaf in Boston (fig. 10, p. 27) are also exceptions.

3. Scholars came to this conclusion regarding the positioning of the reserve heads because one example was found tipped over on its side in the middle of its

burial chamber, near the coffin. See Hassan 1953, 4–5, pls. 3–4a.

4. Lacovara 1997, 28–29.

5. The head illustrated in note 4 above, for example, is missing both ears, and the plaster coating at the back of the head is damaged. It is not possible to attribute the damage to rough handling by thieves because the tomb was discovered in an unplundered state.

6. For overviews of current theories, see Tefnin 1991, *passim*; Roehrig 1999e, 72–78; Millet 1999, 233–34; Lacovara 1997, 28–36; and Junge 1995, 103–9.

7. Reisner 1942, 462, pls. 52a, 46c (*in situ*). Only one other mastaba, G 4440, has been found with two reserve heads (see cat. no. 10).

## 10 | RESERVE HEAD

Dynasty 4, probably reign of Khufu,
2585–2560 B.C.
Giza, tomb G 4440
Limestone
H. 30 cm, w. 21 cm, d. 26 cm
Harvard University-Museum of Fine Arts
Expedition 14.719

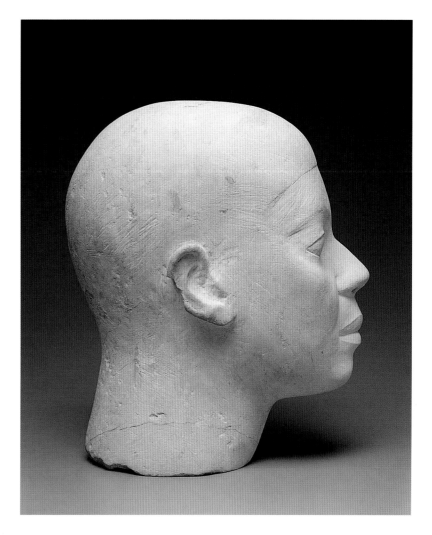

Tomb G 4440 is one of only two tombs discovered with two reserve heads (see cat. no. 9 for one of the heads from the other tomb, G 4140). It is nearly impossible to know whether the pairings were original or created at a later date by intruders.[1] However, because in each tomb one head appeared masculine and one particularly feminine, George Reisner originally hypothesized that each pair represents a husband and wife.[2]

Both of the heads from tomb G 4440 are greater than life size, larger than most other reserve heads.[3] The one illustrated here is in extremely good condition (with only minor chips missing from the ears) and exhibits none of the seemingly deliberate damage of many other reserve heads (see cat. no. 9).[4] Although the full mouth with a large upper lip and upturned nose appear on other examples, this head has many features that distinguish it: prominent cheekbones, wide-set, unusually round eyes, and a profile that projects forward. The face is also broad and substantial with a high forehead accentuated by barely perceptible eyebrows. A short, thick neck that flares at the base supports the considerable volume of the head. Such individualization allows us to gaze at the face of the royal court member for whom this head was created.[5]

Reisner described the reserve heads in 1915 when he wrote that: "[These people] had spoken with Cheops [Khufu] and Chephren [Khafre] and had seen the first and second pyramids in building. Without doubt they had made their offerings in the funerary temple of Cheops [Khufu] and had witnessed the carving of the Great Sphinx."[6]  JLH

1. See Roehrig 1999d, 238–39, fn. 8, for a discussion of this possibility.

2. Reisner 1915, 31–32.

3. For illustrations of both heads from G 4440, see Reisner 1942, pl. 54a, b.

4. The damage to these ears does not appear to be intentional; there are no chisel marks. The other head from this tomb has intentional damage in the form of a roughly cut gouge up the back.

5. See Roehrig 1999d, 239, fn. 2, for other examples of the eye shape and a discussion of a possible Nubian identity.

6. Reisner 1915, 32.

## 11 | PERSONIFIED ESTATES

Dynasty 4, reign of Sneferu to Khufu,
2625–2560 B.C.
Saqqara, north wall of the chapel at
firth 3078
Limestone
H. 46.6 cm, w. 85 cm, d. 2.5 cm
Edwin E. Jack Fund 63.489

This boldly executed scene in raised relief comes from the chapel of a mastaba whose owner's name has been destroyed.[1] It depicts a man and a woman, each carrying a basket of provisions on the head and a pinioned duck in the left hand. The figures would have been advancing toward a large image of the tomb owner to the left. They represent districts or estates, either real or imagined, from which the deceased tomb owner would receive provisions. The personified estates formed an essential part of the mortuary cult, ensuring that offerings were provided for the *ka*, or spirit of the deceased, forever.[2] King Sneferu first utilized this concept in his pyramid chapel with the personification of nomes.[3]

Before each offering bearer on this relief, the name of the district represented is indicated in raised hieroglyphs. Each name ends with a sign composed of two roads crossing, surrounded by a circle, determining that the name is of a place. The woman wearing the classic tripartite hair style and sheath dress represents offerings from a district called Nebutet. The man in a short kilt brings provisions from Senen.[4]  JLH

1. The tomb is located north of the Step Pyramid; see Porter and Moss 1974, 443. The relief comes from side wall D of the mastaba; see Jacquet-Gordon 1962, 331 and fig. 117. Reisner 1936, 364, originally dated the scene to Khufu's reign, but Helen K. Jacquet-Gordon pushes the date back, based on the style of the tomb, to the reign of Sneferu or early in Khufu's reign. For images of the north wall of the entrance, see Smith 1946, pl. 34.

2. Roth 1988c, 52.

3. See Smith 1981, fig. 68, for personified estates from the Bent pyramid at Dashur.

4. These places have not been identified.

## 12 | RELIEF FROM THE TOMB CHAPEL OF KAWAB

Dynasty 4, reign of Khufu, 2585–2560 B.C.
Giza, tomb G 7120
Limestone
H. 55.2 cm, w. 36.8 cm, d. 20.9 cm
Harvard University-Museum of Fine Arts
Expedition 34.59

This relief fragment comes from a chapel in the large double mastaba belonging to Kawab, eldest son of Khufu and perhaps Meretites.[1] Kawab's mastaba was prominently positioned nearest to Khufu's pyramid in the row of tombs to the east. The chapel was one of the first in the Eastern Cemetery to be decorated with reliefs, and its surviving fragments show the herding of oxen, butchering, papyrus preparation, and fowling. Nearby, an image of Kawab would have been positioned on the wall so that it would appear to be viewing these activities.

This fragment was once part of a larger fowling scene.[2] Here, an overseer stands on a skiff, leaning forward on his staff and lifting his left foot slightly.[3] He is dressed in a knee-length kilt and has short hair with a receding hairline. Behind him in the hull is the catch of the day: two cages of birds, five pintail ducks on top, and four different ducks (perhaps wigeons) below. A domesticated heron, used as a decoy to lure other birds, stands on the cages.[4] The decoy suggests that there was likely a clapnet scene nearby. The execution of this relief is competent and clear but lacks fine detail or delicate rendering.  JLH

1. Strudwick 1985a, 147, notes 1–2.

2. Smith 1946, 167, assigned this block to the long east wall of chamber B, the major chamber of the exterior chapel, based on the type of scene and the thickness of the block. For a photograph and line drawing of this fragment, see Simpson 1978, 3, fig. 11g and pl. VId. The other decorated fragments believed to have been part of this chapel are illustrated as figs. 11b–f and pls. VIa–c.

3. See Harpur 1987, fig. 177, for an overseer in a similar pose.

4. For other herons on a skiff from the tomb of Nefermaat in Meidum, see Harpur 1987, fig. 168; for ducks in a box on a boat and herons on the prow, see fig. 120. For a description of herons as decoys in both ancient and modern Egypt, see Houlihan 1986, 13–15.

## 13 | RELIEF OF HEMIUNU

Dynasty 4, reign of Khufu, 2585–2560 B.C.
Giza, tomb G 4000
Limestone
H. 12.1 cm, w. 39.5 cm, d. 7 cm
Harvard University-Museum of Fine Arts
Expedition 27.296

Hemiunu was a high-ranking official of noble lineage. His father, the vizier Nefermaat, was the eldest son of King Sneferu and a builder of pyramids at Dahshur and Meidum. Hemiunu followed in Nefermaat's path, eventually serving as vizier under King Khufu. His most important job in this position was probably the planning and construction of the Great Pyramid and its associated buildings at Giza.

For his own burial, Hemiunu obtained a sizable stone mastaba in the center of the cemetery west of Khufu's pyramid.[1] The tomb's surviving decoration, executed in the high-relief style characteristic of Dynasty 4, is of the finest quality and reinforces the image of Hemiunu as a powerful man of influence. The facial modeling, with its deeply carved eye, soft musculature, and exaggerated nose, is highly individualized.[2] Some scholars have suggested that it approaches portraiture.[3] The fragmentary text to the left of the face is part of a traditional offering formula that begins, "An offering that the king gives…" The relief was part of a scene depicting the deceased seated before a table of bread offerings and comes from the doorway at the entrance of the tomb. YJM

1. Porter and Moss 1974, 122–23.
2. Steindorff 1937, 120–21.
3. Smith 1942, 527.

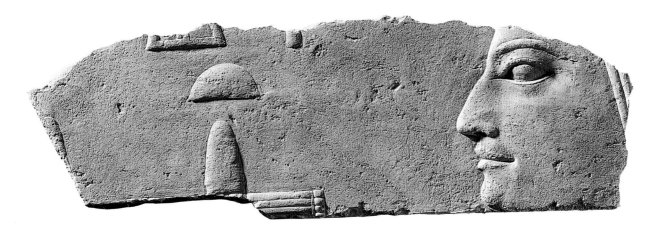

a. Shoulder jar
Dynasty 4, 2625–2500 B.C.
Giza, Menkaure Valley Temple
Egyptian alabaster
H. 17.4 cm, diam. 14.7 cm
Harvard University-Museum of Fine Arts
Expedition 11.604

b. Cylinder jar
Dynasty 4, 2625–2500 B.C.
Giza, tomb G 4240 A
Egyptian alabaster
H. 10.5 cm, diam. 7.1 cm
Harvard University-Museum of Fine Arts
Expedition 21.2617

c. Large bowl
Dynasty 4, 2625–2500 B.C.
Giza, tomb G 4240 A
Egyptian alabaster
H. 10.6 cm, diam. 39.3 cm
Harvard University-Museum of Fine Arts
Expedition 21.2609

d. Cylinder jar
Dynasty 4, 2625–2500 B.C.
Giza, Menkaure Valley Temple
Egyptian alabaster
H. 22.4 cm, diam. 7.3 cm
Harvard University-Museum of Fine Arts
Expedition 11.620

e. Cylinder jar
Dynasty 4, 2625–2500 B.C.
Giza, Menkaure Valley Temple
Egyptian alabaster
H. 15.3 cm, diam. 11.2 cm
Harvard University-Museum of Fine Arts
Expedition 11.514

f. Bowl
Early Dynastic Period, 3000–2675 B.C.
Giza, Menkaure Valley Temple
Siltstone
H. 6.1 cm, diam. 12.3 cm
Harvard University-Museum of Fine Arts
Expedition 11.388

**14** | **OFFERING TABLE WITH ATTACHED STAND**

Dynasty 3, 2675–2625 B.C.
Zawiyet-el-Aryan, Z 500
Egyptian alabaster
H. 9.5 cm, diam. 30.3 cm
Harvard University-Museum of Fine Arts
Expedition 11.2394

Offering tables were customarily placed in the chapel of a mastaba so that relatives, priests, and visitors could deposit offerings for the *ka*, the spirit of the deceased.

This beautifully grained alabaster example was originally found in fragments, but it has been restored to its original shape. It was excavated from a large mudbrick mastaba at Zawiyet-el-Aryan, six kilometers south of Giza, but the exact spot of the find is not known.[1] Clarence Fisher (under the direction of George Reisner) excavated Zawiyet-el-Aryan for only three months, and the records on Z 500 were never fully entered in his diary.[2] We do know that over seventy-five stone vessels and six offering tables were removed from Z 500, most in a fragmentary state. Fisher wrote, "These [stone fragments] are carried to the house every day and are being pieced together as quickly as possible...There are a large number of offering tables, three with low stands or bases attached, the rest simply large discs."[3] This example is one of the round tables mentioned with the slightly flared, low base attached. It replicates a flat disc resting on a ring stand. JLH

1. Porter and Moss 1974, 314; Reisner and Fischer 1911, 59.
2. Dunham 1978, ix, 29.
3. Reisner n.d. d, entry for April 16.

g. Model flat-bottomed basin
Late Dynasty 4 to early Dynasty 5,
2508–2485 B.C.
Giza, tomb G 4631 B
Egyptian alabaster
H. 2.7 cm, diam. 5 cm
Harvard University-Museum of Fine Arts
Expedition 21.3093

h. Opening of the Mouth cup
Dynasty 4, reign of Khufu, 2585–2560 B.C.
Giza, Menkaure Valley Temple
Quartz crystal
H. 4.2 cm, diam. 4.3 cm
Harvard University-Museum of Fine Arts
Expedition 11.770

i. Bowl with recurved rim
Dynasty 4, 2625–2500 B.C.
Giza, Menkaure Valley Temple
Anorthosite gneiss
H. 5.5 cm, diam. 9.8 cm
Harvard University-Museum of Fine Arts
Expedition 11.461

Throughout pharaonic history, finely crafted stone vessels were highly valued symbols of wealth. This group comes from the Giza Necropolis—most are from the Menkaure Valley Temple and the rest are from mastabas of upper class officials. George Reisner found the remains of over six hundred vessels in the valley temple alone. Curiously, many dated to earlier dynasties (cat. no. 15f). Likely these antiques were transferred from older temples during ancient times.[1]

Vessel shapes changed over time, and the types of stone used went in and out of favor as well. For instance, siltstone was used in Predynastic to Early Dynastic times but rarely thereafter. A thick-walled bowl such as catalogue number 15f was a common form for this stone.[2] Anorthosite gneiss was used for vessels from the Early Dynastic through the Old Kingdom periods, and was especially popular for delicate cups or bowls such as catalogue number 15i.[3] Quartz crystal was rare and used primarily for vessels involved in the Opening of the Mouth ritual, performed to give life back to the deceased, during Dynasties 5 and 6. A few date to Dynasty 4 (cat. no. 15h).[4] Egyptian alabaster was the most popular stone; it was

used for many vessel types from the Predynastic period through the Roman era (cat. nos. 15a, d, and e).[5]  JLH

1. The large bowl of catalogue number 15c was found with the cylinder jar, 15b, inside it. Regarding the transfer of antiques to Menkaure's temple and the number of vessels excavated by George Reisner, see Reisner 1931, 103, 180.

2. Stone vessel types are identified in Aston 1994; see pl. 6a for a siltstone example. See Keller 1995, 121, for a siltstone bowl dated to Dynasty 2 that is similar to catalogue number 15f.

3. Catalogue number 50, a Dynasty 6 bowl inscribed for King Teti, is similar to this one. See also Aston 1994, pl. 14b.

4. Catalogue number 15h was found in a ritual set with a peseshkef knife inscribed for King Khufu (cat. no. 17a).

5. Aston 1994, pl. 10a, notes that travertine is the accurate name for the stone that Egyptologists erroneously label as either alabaster or calcite. However, because travertine is not commonly known, we have chosen to use the term "Egyptian alabaster" throughout this text.

## 16 | FOLDED PAD OF INSCRIBED LINEN

Dynasty 4, reign of Menkaure, 2532–2510 B.C.
Giza, tomb G 2220 B
Linen; pigment
H. 24 cm, W. 19 cm, thickness 1.5 cm [folded]

While excavating an intact burial chamber cut into a shaft of a large mastaba in the Western Cemetery, George Reisner found an exceptionally fine cedar coffin and its mummy.[1] The tomb was devoid of funerary goods and textual references that could identify the deceased or the mastaba owner. Within the unadorned coffin, excavators discovered a small, elaborately wrapped body lying on its left side (see photo below).[2] It was padded with linen—over thirty-seven layers of wrapping—to simulate the contours of the human figure.

To give the appearance of the woman in life, the body was fashioned with a padded wig with a twisted tail at the back and a long linen dress with v-neck and shoulder straps. Anatomical features were made of linen as well. Beneath the dress, the breasts, including nipples, were entirely formed of linen, and the legs and feet were individually wrapped.[3] Linen bandages also were modeled on the face to form a perfect nose with nostrils and lips. The eyes and eyebrows were painted, further lending a lifelike quality in death. As in many Old Kingdom attempts to preserve the human form (see cat. no. 47), the body tissues disintegrated beneath these extensive wrappings, leaving primarily skeletal fragments.

On this pad, one of those used to fill out the contours of the body, there is one horizontal line of hieratic text in black ink. As with most linen in offering lists, the descriptive terms relate to the quality of the cloth.[4] This piece is identified as *shemat neferet*, "fine linen." JLH & YJM

1. For a description of the burial, see Reisner 1942, 450–51; Roth 1988d, 76–77.
2. Reisner described the coffin as a "...plain box with flat lid and overlapped bevel-joints." See Reisner 1942, 452.
3. Reisner 1942, 452, provides a summary of the mummy's examination by Dr. Douglas Derry.
4. Smith 1935, 138.

Wrapped mummy of a woman from tomb G 2220 B.

## 17 | MAGICAL *PESESHKEF* KNIVES

a. Knife inscribed for King Khufu
Dynasty 4, reign of Khufu, 2585–2560 B.C.
Giza, Menkaure Valley Temple
Flint
L. 18.3 cm, w. 2.8 cm, d. 0.4 cm
Harvard University-Museum of Fine Arts
Expedition 11.765

b. Fragment of a knife inscribed for Queen
Khamerernebty I
Dynasty 4, reign of Khafre, 2555–2532 B.C.
Giza, Pyramid Temple of Menkaure
Flint
L. 7.2 cm, w. 4.7 cm, d. 0.6 cm
Harvard University-Museum of Fine Arts
Expedition 11.766

*Peseshkef* (*pesesh*, "to divide," and *kef*, "flint,") are sharp-bladed flint ritual knives that had been used in Egypt since Predynastic times. They are sometimes mistakenly referred to as "magic wands." They have long straight shafts and split fishtail tops, and their surfaces are finely ground to a glassy sheen. The listing of *peseshkef* in temple inventories indicates that they were used in such institutions as well as in tombs.[1] The ritual knives have been found in the Menkaure Valley and Pyramid temples as well as in mastabas at Giza.

Recent research has revealed that *peseshkef* were employed as part of Opening of the Mouth ceremonies.[2] Such rebirthing rituals recreated many details of the physical birth process. As the deceased was reborn, the *peseshkef* was used to symbolically cut the umbilical cord, thus separating the child from the mother and giving the child his or her own life. The knife was also held to the mouth to "fix the jaw" so that the child could begin nursing.[3] The ceremony was performed not only on the deceased but also on statues, reliefs, and paintings, in order to bring the depicted figures to life in the next world.

*Peseshkef* were part of ritual sets that usually included six vessels. For example, the complete knife inscribed for King Khufu (cat. no. 17a) was found with a set of stone vessels in the Menkaure Valley Temple.[4] The set was not *in situ*, but the individual objects remained in an order that could be recognized from intact groupings—four small stone cups and two long, narrow-necked stone bottles flanked the knife. The order may have been preserved in the tomb because the ritual set had been kept in a wooden tray that then disintegrated.[5]

The fragment of a much larger knife inscribed for the "mother of the king, Khamerernebty" (cat. no. 17b) was found in the Menkaure Pyramid Temple.[6] Khamerernebty I was a daughter of Khufu, wife of Khafre, and mother of his successor, Menkaure.[7] Both of the inscribed knives were likely antiques at the time they were placed in the temple complex. Apparently, they were saved as sacred equipment. JLH

1. Roth 1992, 116, cites the Abusir papyri, a document that gives extensive details of temple procedure, ritual, and inventory.

2. Roth 1992, 113; Otto 1960, 97–98.

3. Roth 1992, 120, notes that "fix the jaw" comes from Pyramid Text 30. The breasts were then offered to the deceased in the spell after the *peseshkef* knife.

4. The full inscription reads: "The Horus, Medjedu, the King of Upper and Lower Egypt, Khnum Khuf[u]." See Reisner 1931, 233–34, pls. 61e–f, 65a–b.

5. Reisner 1931, 233–34, pls. 61e–f, 65a–b.

6. Reisner 1931, 18, 233, pl. 19a.

7. Baud 1999, 1:192.

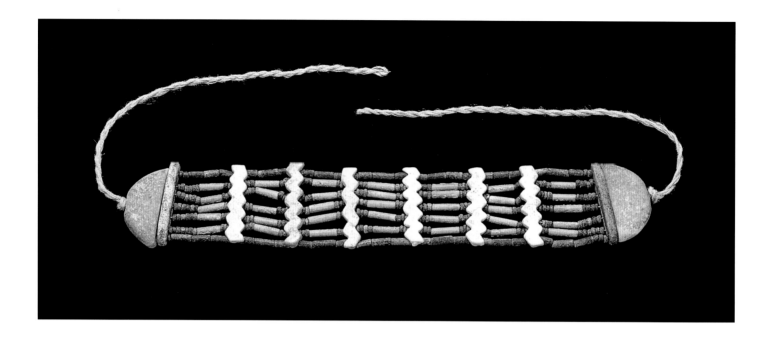

## 18 | CHOKER

Dynasty 4, 2625–2500 B.C.
Giza, tomb G 4341 A
Faience
L. 25 cm, w. 3.8 cm, d. 0.4 cm
Harvard University-Museum of Fine Arts
Expedition 24.1749

Although no complete examples have survived, the neck ornament known as the choker is frequently represented in Old Kingdom sculpture, relief, and paintings. This form of adornment, popular among women of all levels of society during the 4th through 6th Dynasties, was worn both with and without an accompanying broad-collar.[1] Later, it was featured on servant girls of the Middle Kingdom and on coffins of New Kingdom ladies.[2]

Representations of chokers suggest that they were composed of several rows of beads strung between terminals, with a number of spacers in the form of perforated bars to keep the rows in alignment. The elements used in this reconstruction have two interesting features: zigzag-shaped spacers and terminals in two separate parts.[3] The spacers have straight, perforated bars on the underside that facilitate stringing, and wavy surfaces that lie over adjacent beads. The two-part terminals each include a plain, vertical spacer and a semi-circular segment through which the threads are gathered into a single unit for tying. The latter, now buff-colored, may have been glazed in a color that has since disappeared, or perhaps it was gilded.[4] YJM

1. For an analysis of the choker's distribution during the Old Kingdom, see Staehelin 1966, 127.

2. Andrews 1990, 117.

3. The terminal of a collar has two functions. First, it acts as a spacer for the strings of beads to which it is attached, and second, it brings together the various strings that hold the collar in place around the neck.

4. Fragments of gold foil were found in the same location in the tomb.

## 19 | TOOLS

a. Knife
Dynasty 4, reign of Menkaure to Shepseskaf,
2532–2500 B.C.
Giza, Menkaure Valley Temple, room I-332
Flint
L. 20 cm, w. 4 cm, d. 0.5 cm
Harvard University-Museum of Fine Arts
Expedition 11.780

b. Scraper
Dynasty 4, reign of Menkaure to Shepseskaf,
2532–2500 B.C.
Giza, Menkaure Valley Temple, room I-329
Flint
L. 9 cm, w. 5.5 cm, d. 1.4 cm
Harvard University-Museum of Fine Arts
Expedition 11.788

c. Pounder
Mid-Dynasty 4 to Dynasty 5, 2532–2350
B.C.
Giza, street G 7500, south of tomb G 7530 A
Dolorite
H. 18 cm, w. 17 cm, d. 8 cm
Harvard University-Museum of Fine Arts
Expedition 27.1549

Reisner identified six types of flint implements from the Menkaure temples. He regarded these flints, which included the straight-backed knife with handle (cat. no. 19a) and the triangular scraper (cat. no. 19b), as traditional burial items exhibiting rough workmanship. His explanation for the lack of quality is based on the observation that copper implements had begun to replace flint tools during the Old Kingdom.[1] Yet flint tools remained symbolically important even when they were no longer prized for their artistry or efficacy. The knife, for example, derives from finely chipped Predynastic cutting tools that were used in the sacrificial slaughter of animals. However, by Dynasty 4, knife blades included in burials were thick, coarse, and dull with pointed tips and straight handles.[2]

Another stone tool used for cutting, scraping, and boring, was the pointed flint. Within this category are triangular forms worked on one plane with one or more sharpened edge. Excavators recovered several summarily worked examples from the Menkaure Valley Temple's magazines.

Pear-shaped dolorite pounders (cat. no. 19c) were used as hammer stones in the quarrying of hard rocks such as granite. Depending on size, they were either held in both hands or hafted onto wooden handles. Once worn, they could be recycled into rollers for moving heavy objects such as sarcophagi.[3]  YJM

1. The finest flintwork was produced during the Late Predynastic and Early Dynastic periods. See Spencer 1980, 91–101. Metal played an increasingly important role in daily life, but flint implements such as knives, scrapers, chisels, saws, and drills were used throughout the pharaonic period. See Nicholson and Shaw 2000, 28–29.

2. Earlier knives had curved, concave handles and curved tips.

3. Lehner 1997, 207, 210–11.

# Dynasty 5

Fig. 36
Relief scene featuring starving bedouins, from the causeway of the pyramid of King Unas at Saqqara, Dynasty 5.

Fig. 37
Pyramid Texts from the antechamber of the pyramid of King Unas at Saqqara, Dynasty 5.

A shortage of source material leaves several gaps in what is understood about the royal succession from the 4th to the 5th Dynasty. The first known 5th Dynasty king is Userkaf, and the prevailing theory holds that he founded the dynasty with Queen Khentkawes, the last ruler of Dynasty 4.[1] It is certain that Userkaf's sons succeeded him and that the new royal family chose to return to the Saqqara-Abusir area to build their tombs and temples, reducing Giza's role as a royal necropolis. The move most likely was due to a combination of factors that included family rivalry, a new source of suitable limestone, lack of space on the Giza plateau, and close proximity to the capital city.[2]

The kings and queens of Dynasty 5 encouraged significant architectural innovation, and the ground plans and decorative programs for their royal pyramid complexes became prototypes for other tombs in Dynasties 5 and 6.[3] Some new features reflected shifts in religious emphases, such as the creation of a temple complex for open-air cult ceremonies to worship Re as both the sun and creator god.[4] Both Re and Osiris, the god of the netherworld, became more prominent at this time. By the end of Dynasty 5, King Unas's pyramid included stone-carved passages from the Pyramid Texts describing the deceased king's travel to the next world where he would be reborn as Osiris and join Re in his daily journey through the heavens (fig. 37).[5]

Because the 5th Dynasty's rulers continued to build pyramid complexes while maintaining the funerary cults of their ancestors, an increasing number of priestly and secular personnel were required by the state. An important consequence of this trend was a burgeoning class of bureaucrats who could afford to build and decorate private tombs. The sheer numbers, as well as the wealth, of this official, elite class helped to spur originality and variety in the sculptural arts.

With new genres of relief and sculpture came a fresh liveliness and naturalistic style. Among royal reliefs, innovative scenes included victories, foreigners, captives, views of shipping and markets, the seasons of the year, and even famine victims (fig 36).[6] Private tomb relief, too, saw an important evolution as images from life came to decorate the inner offering room of chapels.[7] Such reliefs depicted men at work in the fields, on the river, and laboring in all types of workshops for the first time (fig. 13, p. 29). In sculpture, pseudogroups, freestanding statues with more than one image of the same person, were introduced,[8] and figures of children were added to pair statues of parents

(fig. 33, p. 45). Servant statues (introduced in Dynasty 4) also became more popular and were shown performing a greater variety of tasks (cat. no 31). However, with few exceptions (cat. no. 25), sculptures are smaller in scale than those of Dynasty 4.

Another hallmark of Dynasty 5 was the copious record keeping in which the state was engaged. Edicts (cat. no. 21), king lists, and temple accounts abound from this period, reflecting a large bureaucracy whose membership and political influence were gradually expanding. More and more, its officials were able to appropriate prerogatives formerly reserved for royal relatives. Even the important position of vizier now could be held by non-royal officials. At the same time, some nomarchs were choosing to be buried in their own provinces rather than near their sovereigns. A few of these local governors even dared to deify themselves in their own tombs.[9] The power of those serving the king was growing, and the decentralization that would ultimately bring a close to the Old Kingdom had commenced. JLH

1. Baud 1999, 2:546–52, notes that there are multiple interpretations as to her parents and children. See also Lehner 1997, 138. Krejčí 2000, 474, suggests that the royal family was divided into two or more parties struggling for control.

2. Krejčí 2000, 473–74.

3. Arnold 1997, 63, 71. Krejčí 2000, 475, also notes that Sahure's pyramid complex became the standard followed for pyramid complexes of Dynasties 5 and 6.

4. Lehner 1997, 150. The only precedent is the temple of the great Sphinx at Giza dedicated to the sun. See also Krejčí 2000, 472, who notes that six kings of Dynasty 5 built sun temples but only two have been found.

5. Lehner 1997, 154. While the pyramid of King Unas at Saqqara was the first to incorporate Pyramid Text decoration inside the pyramid's burial chamber, the Pyramid Texts were already very old by this time.

6. A number of complete reliefs from royal funerary temples of Dynasty 5 have been preserved, whereas those of Dynasty 4 have survived only in small fragments.

7. Smith 1946, 189.

8. Eaton-Krauss, 1995, 61. She gives an additional characteristic of pseudogroups on p. 57 as "each could be divided into at least two separate statues of the owner without damaging any figure included in the composition."

9. Hornung 1999, 38, notes that the official Izi in Edfu and Hekaib in Elephantine were worshiped as gods until the Middle Kingdom.

## 20 SEATED STATUE OF AKHMERETNESUT

Mid-Dynasty 5 to early Dynasty 6, 2455–2338 B.C.
Giza, tomb G 2184
Limestone
H. 68.5 cm, w. 24.7 cm, d. 45.5 cm
Harvard University-Museum of Fine Arts Expedition 12.1482

Akhmeretnesut was "overseer of the department of those foremost of the royal precinct."[1] This title reveals that he oversaw a group called the *khentiu-she* in the king's palace. *Khentiu-she* served the king either in the palace or in his mortuary cult and included all classes of workers from farmers to high officials.[2] Because the first written example of the term occurs during King Nyuserre's reign (2455–2425 B.C.), the title provides the earliest possible set of dates for Akhmeretnesut.[3]

This seated statue was found set into the floor of Akhmeretnesut's mastaba chapel next to a large offering basin (see photo at right). The mastaba has a complex architectural history with three distinct building phases—evidence suggests that the tomb was enlarged and refaced during its owner's career. In its earliest state, it had a simple one-room chapel, now identified as chamber A, with two false doors. Later, a second chamber, B, and a courtyard, C, were added. This statue and its offering table come from chamber B. Akhmeretnesut's tomb has been dated widely, but both the inscriptional evidence and the style of the relief and architecture indicate a range from mid-Dynasty 5 to early Dynasty 6.[4]

The statue was carved as a single unit on a backless seat. Its solid figure has a commanding presence with stocky arms and legs in the style of the time.[5] However in contrast, his open hand has long, smooth delicate fingers that lie flat on his lap. The face is finely carved with round cheeks, full lips, and large eyes accented by a double-carved line on the upper lid. There is an unexplained pinkish red color on the broken surfaces of the nose, mouth, and chin, possibly representing ancient repairs.[6] Traces of original red pigment remain on the legs and torso, and blue-green is visible at the edges of the crisply carved hieroglyphs on the base. The space between the calves was left rough and painted black. The shoulder-length, striated hair-

style is parted in the middle and swept back, flaring at the sides. His wrap-around kilt with pleated panel is secured with a tied knot. The end of the tie, also pleated, sticks up above the belt. JLH

1. Lehner 1997, 234–35. Jones 2000, 1:241, title no. 882, offers an older translation: "overseer of the department of tenant-landholders of the Great House."

2. Lehner 1997, 234–35.

3. Ann Macy Roth provided this date by personal communication. Previously, the earliest attested occurrence was during the reign of King Djedkare Isesi (2415–2371 B.C.); see also Lehner 1997, 234, and Baud 1996, 21.

4. Baud 1996, 40–41, dates it from King Menkaure of Dynasty 4 to King Nyuserre of Dynasty 5; Cherpion 1989, 123, note 257, claims Dynasty 4; Harpur 1987, 265, note 8, Dynasty 5 (King Unas) to Dynasty 6 (King Teti); Baer 1960, 52, end of Dynasty 5 or later. See also Reisner 1942, 380–81; Smith 1946, 198–99. Roth 1988a, 83–87, dates the tomb to late Dynasty 5 or Dynasty 6.

5. Metropolitan Museum of Art 1999, 372–75, shows seated figures of Nikare with similar proportions, heavy legs, and detailed knees, which date to King Nyuserre or later.

6. Pink stucco fill was often used for ancient repairs. I would like to thank Susanne Gänsicke, Associate Conservator, and Kent Severson, Contract Conservator, of the Conservation and Collections Management Department of the Museum of Fine Arts, Boston, for this information.

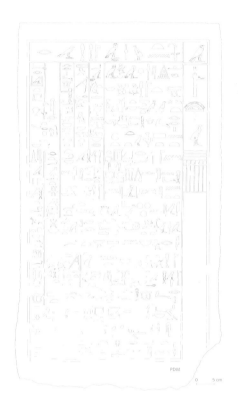

## 21 DECREE OF NEFERIRKARE

Dynasty 5, reign of Neferirkare Kakai,
2472–2462 B.C.
Abydos
Limestone
H. 106.3 cm, w. 65 cm, d. 26 cm
Gift of the Egyptian Exploration
Fund 1903 03.1896

This royal decree was erected for King
Neferirkare Kakai near the Temple of Osiris in
Abydos.[1] It is addressed to Overseer of Priests
Hemwer, the highest-ranking priest of the day.[2]
We know that it was originally on papyrus
because its text tells us that it was put in writing
and that "the king himself was present at the
sealing on the second month of summer, day
11."[3]

The edict's function was to free Abydos's
priests, especially those of the Temple of Osiris,
from forced labor for the nome. With it, the
king placed limits on the growing power of local
noblemen and officials headed by the nomarch.
(Such locally based powers would, at the end of
the Old Kingdom, usurp all political control.)
The king decreed that they could not press
priests or priestly staff into service for the
nome's large building projects or agricultural

endeavors, exempting the priests from any such
compulsory work "for the length of eternity."
The priests' only job, the king notes, was to
maintain the temples and make them prosper.
Any official who did not obey the edict would
meet harsh penalties: the loss of all possessions
and forced hard labor.[4] JLH

1. Excavated by W. M. Flinders Petrie; see Petrie
1903, 42–43. See also Porter and Moss 1937, 40.

2. Ranke 1935, 239. Also, according to Petrie 1903,
42, the title belonged to the head of the local temple
administration. In fact, the nomarch himself might
combine the religious title with his civil duties.

3. Leprohon 1985, 49. Also published in Goedicke
1967, *passim*.

4. The punishment included "the loss of their house,
field, people and everything in their possession and
they would be put into hard labor." Leprohon 1985,
49.

## 22 | SEAL OF OFFICE

Dynasty 5, reign of Djedkare Isesi,
2415–2371 B.C.
Reportedly from Northwest Anatolia
Gold
H. 6.4 cm, diam. 2.9 cm
Centennial Gift of Landon T. Clay 68.115

Cylinder seals bearing royal and private names with titles are known from both the Early Dynastic Period and the Old Kingdom.[1] They are typically made of stone, but there are also some examples fabricated from gold and silver. Among those, however, a sound context is rare.[2] The provenance of this seal—unique in its size and state of preservation—is uncertain.[3]

The seal is classified as a "seal of office," which is always anonymous. It contains the

name of the reigning king, Djedkare Isesi, and official titles, but no personal name.[4] When the office represented by the titles was passed on to a successor, the seal was handed over to that individual, but when the king's reign changed, the seal was no longer valid.[5] Cylinder seals of this type were used to identify documents, boxes, provisions, and even doors.[6] A relief from the pyramid temple of King Sahure at Abusir illustrates their standard form during the Old Kingdom: long, with a biconcave body (see illustration at left).[7]

While most precious metal examples are made from sheet metal with a chased surface decoration over a core, this piece stands out because it was constructed of cast cylinders that were subsequently decorated. The gold from which the cylinder was created has a high copper content, suggesting to some scholars that it was not of Old Kingdom date. However, with recent analysis of excavated gold samples from Giza, it can now be shown that the copper content is within the normal range for that time and place. For a detailed discussion of the inscription, construction, and materials of this seal, see Appendix B. YJM & JLH

1. For Early Dynastic examples of cylinder seals and seal impressions bearing royal and private names recovered from the mastaba tombs at Helwan (opposite Saqqara), see Saad 1969, 18–19, 22–23, 27, 67, pls. 174–76; for the largest group of provenanced cylinder seals from this period, see Reisner 1908, 150–51, pls. 9, 43–44. For a comprehensive listing of cylinder seals dating to the Old Kingdom, see Kaplony 1977 and 1981, *passim*.

2. For a gold Early Dynastic cylinder seal from Naga ed-Deir (N 1532), see Reisner 1908, 151, pls. 9c–d. For a silver cylinder seal inscribed for King Khafre from Menkaure's valley temple (MFA 11.962), see Reisner 1931, 234, pl. 64-l. For an unprovenanced gold cylinder seal inscribed for King Menkaure, see Schäfer 1910, 15, pls. 2, 7; Kaplony 1981, 102, no. 9, pl. 33; and Müller and Thiem 1999 70–71, fig. 142.

3. This gold seal was said to come from a cache of gold objects in Northwest Anatolia. For a discussion of Anatolian connections, see Young 1972, 11–12.

4. Kaplony 1977, 10, calls this seal type, "Amtssiegel." Kaplony 1981, pl. 92, no. 38, publishes this seal.

5. Kaplony 1983, 295.

6. We are grateful to John Nolan for his insights on the uses of cylinder seals in the Old Kingdom.

7. By comparison, Early Dynastic seals have truncated cylinder forms.

## 23 | LINTEL FROM THE TOMB OF NEFER

Late Dynasty 5, about 2400 B.C.
Giza, debris of tomb G 1461
Limestone
L. 85 cm, diam. 20.4 cm
Harvard University-Museum of Fine Arts
Expedition 21.3080

Inscribed stone drums were sometimes installed above the entranceways of Egyptian tombs. These architectural elements originate in the wooden logs used in the mudbrick mastabas of earlier dynasties.[1] This example, found in the debris of a tomb in Giza's Western Cemetery, is inscribed for an official named Nefer whose tomb has not been located.[2] However, we know from the centrally placed inscription carved in raised relief that he was "overseer of scribes and keeper of the secret matters of the pyramid of Khufu, the one who is provided for by his lord, the overseer of the treasury, Nefer."[3]

The most important of Nefer's duties was that of senior executive of the state's treasury. In this position, he was responsible for the daily activities of the department and would have operated under the direct supervision of the vizier. His other titles, including the one that names Khufu's pyramid, were most likely honorific, lower-ranking offices.[4] Nefer's epithets, along with certain paleographic forms, provide important dating information.[5] They place him somewhere in the latter part of Dynasty 5, when high-ranking officials often chose to be buried at Giza.[6] YJM

1. Sanborn 1922, 27.
2. Porter and Moss 1974, 64.
3. Strudwick 1985b, 43–44. See also Strudwick 1985a, 109, 277, 281, 283. This Nefer is not to be confused with the one of tomb G 2110, a 4th Dynasty overseer of the treasury. See Smith 1946, 163, note 1.
4. Strudwick 1985a, 283–84.
5. Strudwick 1985b, 50–51.
6. Those who held offices in Khufu's cult at Giza were particularly likely to be buried there.

## 24 | FALSE DOOR OF INTY

Early to mid-Dynasty 5, 2500–2455 B.C.
Giza, street G 7700 in the *radim* east of tomb G 7753
Limestone
H. 121.2 cm, w. 62.5 cm, d. 19 cm
Harvard University-Museum of Fine Arts
Expedition 31.781

This false door inscribed for Inty, a priestess of Hathor, was found in the *radim* (fill) of street G 7700, but Inty's tomb has never been located.[1] Without an architectural context or associated grave goods, the false door can be dated only by stylistic means. Several features lead scholars to place it from early to mid-Dynasty 5: the lack of cavetto cornice or torus molding, the presence of two pairs of jambs, and the high-relief style.[2] In addition, the manner in which Inty holds the lotus (grasping it near the calyx with her whole hand and not with her fingertips) has not been attested before Dynasty 5.[3] The inscription provides further support for a Dynasty 5 date because it mentions the god Osiris, a practice not likely to have been in use before that time.[4]

Inty's name is found only once on the false door, on the panel. She is seated on a stool smelling a lotus, and the four signs that comprise her name are placed before her. They cleverly take the shape and space normally occupied by the table piled with offerings. Inty's titles, "royal acquaintance and priestess of Hathor" and "lady of the sycamore," are listed on the lintel. Curiously, the place where Inty's name should appear after the titles has been left uncarved. Some have suggested that the false door was prefabricated and not inscribed until after purchase.[5] However, the fine quality of the carving and the high status of the titles make this unlikely. One wonders why the ancient artist neglected to write the owner's name, the most important of all inscriptions.

The inner and outer jambs bear the same texts in near mirror images. The two outer jamb formulas are to Anubis, requesting that Inty be buried as a revered one before the great god. The prayers inscribed on the two inner jambs are to Osiris; no epithets are given. They ask that invocation offerings be made for Inty at every festival, every day. JLH

1. Reisner n.d. g, field number 29-12-106; Porter and Moss 1974, 203.

2. Strudwick 1985a, 15–16, 35–36.

3. Harpur 1987, 134, pl. 9.

4. Bolshakov 1992, 203–10, suggests that the first writing of Osiris dates to mid-Dynasty 5. He disputes the evidence presented in Begelsbacher-Fischer 1981, 121, note 2, that the first mention of Osiris occurred between late Dynasty 4 and early Dynasty 5.

5. Manuelian 1998a, 115–27, discusses this theory.

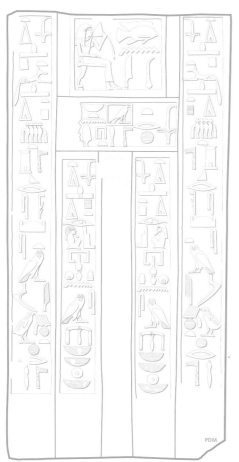

## 25 STANDING FIGURES OF BABAEF

a. Babaef
Late Dynasty 4 to early Dynasty 5,
2508–2485 B.C.
Giza, tomb G 5230
Limestone
H. 147.3 cm, w. 36.5 cm, d. 62.5 cm
Harvard University-Museum of Fine Arts
Expedition 21.953a–b

b. Babaef
Late Dynasty 4 to early Dynasty 5,
2508–2485 B.C.
Giza, tomb G 5230
Limestone
H. 140.3 cm, w. 30.4 cm, d. 67.3 cm
Harvard University-Museum of Fine Arts
Expedition 21.955a–b

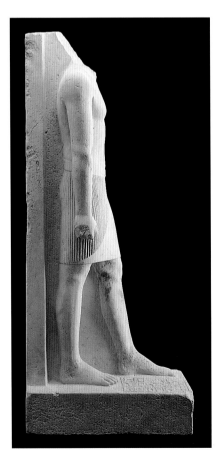

Babaef's tomb complex, located in Giza's Western Cemetery opposite the pyramid of Khufu, is unique in having two symmetrically placed serdab houses built in front of the mastaba.[1] Each of these structures contains a transverse offering chamber near the entrance with windows revealing four narrow spaces in the building's core (see illustration below).[2] Several dozen seated and standing statues of the deceased, of varying size and form and carved from an assortment of stones, were excavated from these channels.[3] At least two sculptures are pseudogroups, freestanding statues with multiple images of the same individual.[4]

Six of the limestone statues excavated, including the two here, are complete except for their heads and feature a youthful, athletic Babaef standing with arms against his sides, hands closed, and left foot forward. These idealized representations are nearly life-size and are distinguished by their attire—either a short kilt with pleated flap and knotted belt or knee-length skirt with apron. All have back pillars and are inscribed on the base with the owner's name and titles. While these sculptures may appear at first glance to be uniform, close examination reveals subtle differences in the modeling of the arms, legs, and torsos. Considering the quantity of statues made, it is likely that several artists were involved in the final steps of production. Traces of red and black pigment survive on the extremities and base, a reminder that Egyptian statuary was typically painted.

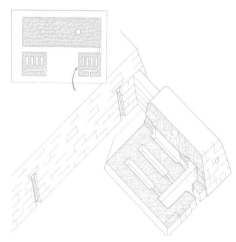

Reconstruction drawing of the serdab
in front of the mastaba of Babaef.

Although Babaef's tomb was undecorated, its size and complexity provide testimony to his elevated status and importance. The text carved into the base of these two statues identifies him as a vizier—the state's chief civil administrator. It also claims that he held the title of "prince," although this designation may have been merely honorific.[5] Unfortunately, the name of the king under whom Babaef served is not mentioned; scholars generally believe that he lived during the reign of King Shepseskaf, the last ruler of Dynasty 4. On other sculptures from the tomb, the inscription reads "prince, overseer of all construction projects for the king," perhaps referring to an office held prior to that of vizier.[6] In that capacity, Babaef would have been responsible for major architectural and engineering programs. YJM

1. Porter and Moss 1974, 155–57.

2. Dieter Arnold 1999, 46.

3. The estimate is that there were about thirty to fifty statues of the vizier, many of them fragmentary. See Smith 1946, 50–51.

4. One is a red-granite statuette with two standing figures; the other, also of red granite, features two seated figures. The standing pair is the first known example of its type. For a discussion of pseudogroups, see Eaton-Krauss 1995.

5. Strudwick 1985a, 82–83.

6. A sculpture in the Vienna Kunsthistorisches Museum, Ägyptisch-Orientalische Sammlung collection (number ÄS 7785) bears this title; see Ziegler 1999b, 298.

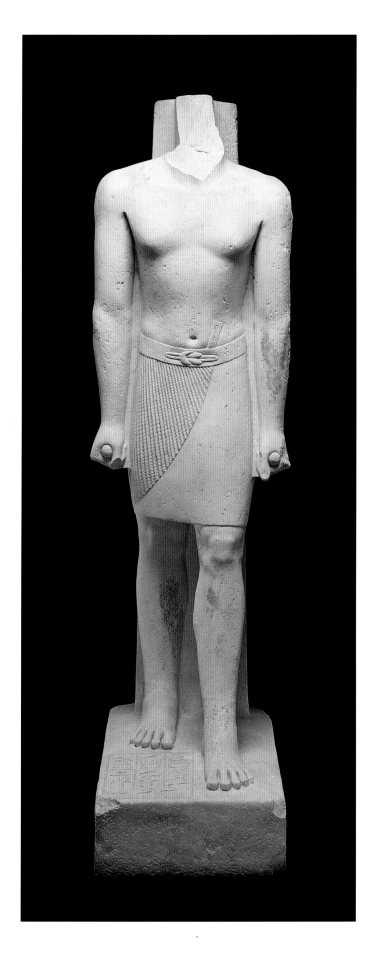

## 26 | BABAEF REPRESENTED AS A SCRIBE

Late Dynasty 4 to early Dynasty 5,
2508–2485 B.C.
Giza, tomb G 5230
Black granite
H. 36 cm, w. 25.2 cm, d. 19 cm
Harvard University–Museum of Fine Arts
Expedition 21.931a–c

The mastaba tomb of Babaef housed numerous
statues of the important official (see cat. no. 25),
but this sculpture was recovered from a nearby
pit where plunderers had discarded it.[1] Hieroglyphs along the front of the base identify
Babaef as the subject. In contrast to standing
figures in which the emphasis is on the owner's
youthful, athletic physique, this seated representation distinguishes Babaef as a man of wisdom
and learning. He is depicted as a scribe with legs
crossed and an open papyrus roll across his lap.
A palette with cakes of red and black ink rests
in his left hand while his right thumb and fore-
finger are joined as if holding a reed brush. The
head is bent forward slightly and the body leans
toward the right so that it appears oddly asym-
metrical, but overall the posture is one of con-
centrated energy. Babaef wears a flared wig with
a central part and the features of his round face
are softly modeled into a reflective, otherworldly
expression. This impression of Babaef as a sage
elder is reinforced by the minimally rendered
musculature of the upper torso and the creases
of the face. YJM

1. Porter and Moss 1974, 155–57

## 27 | PTAHIRANKH AND NYANKHHATHOR

Dynasty 5, reign of Neferirkare to
Reneferef, 2472–2455 B.C.
Giza, tomb G 1501
Red granite
H. 49.2 cm, w. 32.7 cm, d. 31.4 cm
Harvard University-Museum of Fine Arts
Expedition 12.1488

Recovered from the far-western edge of the Giza
necropolis, this statue depicts a couple seated on
a bench with a back slab that rises to the neck-
line.[1] Both figures are summarily carved with
greater attention afforded the heads. Their faces
are remarkably alike, with full cheeks, raised
eyebrows, eyelid folds, broad noses, and well-
defined mouths. The material and block form,
as well as the thick necks, short waists, and
heavy ankles, lend a sense of containment and
inner focus to the sculpture.

   The man, identified by an inscription on his
lap as "the steward Ptahirankh," is seated to
the left of his spouse. He wears a short, tightly
curled wig that covers his ears and extends to
the base of the neck, a style popularized during
Dynasty 4.[2] The modeling of the arms, legs, and
torso is subtle and the pleats of the short, belted
kilt are barely visible. The name and title of the
woman, "the king's acquaintance, Nyankhhathor," is also provided by text carved into the
figure's lap. She is only slightly smaller than her
spouse and is shown wearing a plain, sheath
dress that ends at the ankles. Her medium-
length wig is composed of twisted locks parted
in the middle and arranged in vertical rows.[3]
In a gesture of simple affection, Nyankhhathor
encircles her husband's waist with her left arm.
YJM

1. Porter and Moss 1974, 64–65. See also Smith
1946, 74.

2. It has been suggested that this style dates to the
reign of King Nyuserre or earlier. See Cherpion 1998,
104–5.

3. Natural hair, in the form of horizontal bands
across the forehead, is also visible. For this feature as
a Dynasty 5 dating device, see Cherpion 1998, 101.

## 28 | SEATED STATUE OF NYSHEPSESNESUT

Dynasty 5, 2500–2350 B.C.
Giza, tomb G 4410
Limestone
H. 38 cm, w. 11.5 cm, d. 23 cm.
Harvard University-Museum of Fine Arts
Expedition 21.352

Nyshepsesnesut was a minor official whose titles were *ka* priest, overseer of linen, and manicurist.[1] However this statue of him, with names and titles incised on the sides and back, was found in a tomb belonging to another, higher official.[2] Nyshepsesnesut was likely related to the tomb owner or perhaps employed by him as a priest.[3] The inclusion of such a priest's statue would thereby enable the tomb owner to receive eternal services for his funerary cult.[4] At the same time, the lower-ranking Nyshepsesnesut would have considered it a great favor.

Nyshepsesnesut is seated on a backless throne with both hands on his thighs, the right grasping an unidentified object. His short hairstyle is composed of concentric rows of curls that cover his ears. The diminutive nose and mouth and smooth round cheeks lend a youthful sweetness to the face. This aspect is also emphasized by the prominent eyes and lightly modeled eyebrow ridges. The body, too, appears soft, as it lacks defined musculature. Much of the original pigment remains on the sculpture, especially the red-brown on the body and the black on the seat, base, and wig. Traces of a painted broadcollar are also visible. JLH

1. The title *ir 'nwt* is translated here as "manicurist." Moussa and Altenmüller 1977, 29, cites the title "the king's manicurist" for both the officials Khnumhotep and Niankhkhnum. Faulkner 1962, 43, translates *'nwt* as either toenail or finger nail, so scholars have interpreted the title as manicurist or pedicurist. Reeder 1993, 25, notes that the unusual sign used to write this title is the animal paw with extended claws. The more common hieroglyph in the Middle Kingdom is the horizontal human finger; see Gardiner 1982, D51.

2. The text inscribed on the left side of the seat is oriented in the opposite direction of the figure. Customarily, the hieroglyphs are oriented in the same direction as the figure, as is the case on the right side of the seat. Reisner 1942, 514, found this statuette and that of another priest, Isiankh, as well as a pottery bowl, in an offering room of a small mudbrick serdab only forty centimeters high. See Porter and Moss 1974, 127.

3. Simpson 1977, 14; Reisner 1942, 514.

4. Russmann 1989, 32.

## 30 PAIR STATUE FROM THE TOMB OF WERI

Mid- to late Dynasty 5, reign of Nyuserre
to Unas, 2455–2350 B.C.
Giza, tomb G 2415
Limestone
H. 56.5 cm, w. 29.2 cm, d. 17.8 cm
Harvard University-Museum of Fine Arts
Expedition 21.2596

Eleven statuettes were found in the serdab associated with the mastaba tomb of Weri and Meti
(cat. nos. 29, 31).[1] Two from the grouping,
including this unidentified couple, were pair
statues. Although lacking an inscription, the
figures probably represent close relatives of the
deceased.[2]

The overall contour of this sculpture deviates
from the standard block form of 5th Dynasty
sculpture. The husband and wife lean outward,
creating an inverted pyramid, and the rectangular slab behind the couple ends at the woman's
shoulders so that both heads are sculpted in the
round. The man is in the typical striding position, with arms at his sides and left foot
advanced. He wears a short, curled wig that
conceals his ears and a kilt with a stiff, triangular apron. His broad shoulders, muscled torso,
and slim waist suggest a youthful athleticism
while his forward gaze is distant and otherworldly.

The woman stands slightly apart from her
mate, leaving an area of negative space between
her torso and her husband's left arm. In a manner typical of the 5th Dynasty, one arm extends
around her husband's shoulders while the hand
of the other rests near the crook of his elbow.[3]
Her curled, shoulder-length wig is parted in the
middle and a band of natural hair is visible
along the upper forehead. The sheath dress is
close fitting and ends above the ankles where
remnants of painted anklets may be seen. It is
likely that she was once adorned with matching
wrist ornaments and a beaded broadcollar. YJM

1. Porter and Moss 1974, 93.
2. Smith 1960, 56.
3. Labbé-Toutée and Ziegler 1999, 378–79.

## 31 | WOMAN HEATING BREAD MOLDS

Dynasty 5, 2500–2350 B.C.
Giza, tomb G 2415
Limestone
H. 23.8 cm, w. 12.5 cm, d. 32 cm
Harvard University–Museum of Fine Arts
Expedition 21.2600

By the middle of Dynasty 5, statuettes depicting people engaged in daily life activities were included in the mastaba tombs of officials. These figures were often placed, along with statues of the tomb owner, within a closed, inaccessible chamber of the serdab. This room was typically located behind the false door and featured one or two window-like slots at eye level.

For many years, it was thought that these three-dimensional figures represented servants on a nobleman's estate. In this capacity, they would be magically transformed into workers who would provide life-sustaining services to the tomb owner in the afterlife.[1] More recently, Ann Macy Roth has designated these objects as "serving statuettes." In this interpretation, the figures portray highly placed personages rather than anonymous servants. In fact, an analysis of inscribed examples suggests they were often the relatives, friends, and retainers of the deceased. These relations are shown engaged in useful,

humble tasks as a demonstration of their piety. Their inclusion in the serdab, positioned so that their gazes are directed toward the openings, insured access to the next world and allowed them to be beneficiaries of certain revitalizing rituals such as censing.[2]

This serving statuette was recovered from the tomb of a man named Weri (cat. nos. 29, 30) and his wife Meti, along with another of a kneeling woman grinding corn.[3] Here, the female figure heats *bedja* pots, bell-shaped vessels of clay used for bread making, over an open fire.[4] Seated on the ground with right leg bent under and left leg raised and bent at the knee, she stokes a fire with a stick while protecting her face and wig from the glare of the embers with her hand. The figure wears a short skirt and a cloth covers the crown of a curled wig. Although the woman's posture implies agility, her pendulous breasts suggest advancing age.[5] A break in the middle of the base appears to have been repaired in ancient times. As with many stone sculptures of the period, the statuette was once completely painted. Fortunately, a considerable amount of the original pigment remains—yellow on exposed skin; black on the wig, eyes, vessels, and base; and red covering the stacked, conical pots. Less visible are the black outlines of a necklace with pendant and ornaments on the wrist.[6] YJM

1. See Breasted 1948.

2. I would like to thank Ann Macy Roth for her insights on these statuettes by personal communication, May 10, 2000.

3. For a description of tomb G 2415, see Reisner 1942, 253. Five additional limestone sculptures were found there: three standing male figures and two pair statues. There were also traces of at least four wooden bases from statues that had decayed. See Porter and Moss 1974, 93; also Smith 1946, 74–75.

4. Statuettes of men and women heating bread molds are paralleled in relief representations. The Dynasty 5 tomb of Djaty (G 2337 X), for example, contained a relief of his daughters making bread, bearing offerings, and brewing beer (line drawing below); see Simpson 1980, 28–30, pl. 41.

5. For a further description of this figure, as well as another example of a baker heating bread molds, see Breasted 1948, 28–29, pl. 28.

6. The jewelry and curled wig on a recently discovered statuette of a woman grinding grain (Giza G 7) has been cited as evidence that the woman represented is not a servant but the lady of the house. See Hawass 1995a, 91–95, pls. 31–32.

Line drawing of a relief from the tomb of Djaty (G 2337 X) featuring his daughters making bread, bearing offerings, and brewing beer.

## 32 | OFFERING BASIN FOR KHNUMU

Mid- to late Dynasty 5, 2500–2350 B.C.
Giza, tomb G 2009 A
Limestone
L. 36.6 cm, h. 13.3 cm, d 21.9 cm
Harvard University-Museum of Fine Arts
Expedition  06.1884

Basins were often set before a tomb's false door with rims flush with the ground (see photo at right).[1] The shape was designed for receiving funerary libations such as water, beer, wine, or milk.[2] Here, crisp hieroglyphs on the flat rim request non-liquid offerings as well:

> An offering that the King and Anubis, who is foremost of the divine booth, give: a very fine burial in the necropolis and possessor of veneration before the great god for the royal servant Khnumu. May his invocation offerings of bread, beer, fowl and oxen be made every day, at monthly and bimonthly festivals, for the royal servant Khnumu.[3]

With this prayer, eternal offerings were ensured for the spirit of the tomb owner.

The only title provided for Khnumu is *khentiu-she*, "those foremost of the royal precinct" (see cat. no. 20). The *khentiu-she* either performed personal services for the living king in the palace or they served in the mortuary cult of the deceased king.[4]  JLH

1. For a similar offering basin found sunk in the ground, see Thomas 1995, 135, no. 46. For an identical offering basin from tomb G 2009 inscribed for Semerka and now in Cairo (JE 38674), see Lehmann 1995, 25, 46–47, pl. 22. Lehmann notes that Semerka's basin is *in situ* in the photograph. Khnumu's may be seen in the foreground of the same photograph, upside-down.

2. Abou-Ghazi 1980, 9–10.

3. The text runs from upper right to left and down to the lower left corner. It resumes in the right hand column and runs down and across to the lower left corner.

4. Lehmann 1995, 46–47, identifies eight individuals in tomb G 2009 who have this title. For details of this title, see also Jones 2000, 691–92; Lehner 1997, 234–35; Baud 1996, 13–38; Roth 1991a, *passim*.

## 33 | CANOPIC JARS AND LIDS

Dynasty 5, 2500–2350 B.C.
Giza, tomb G 7249 A
Limestone
a. H. 25.2 cm with lid, diam. 14.5cm
b. H. 24.5 cm with lid, diam. 14.3 cm
c. H. 25 cm with lid, diam. 14.8 cm
d. H. 25 cm (no lid), diam. 15 cm
Harvard University-Museum of Fine Arts
Expedition 27.1553.1–4

During the mummification process, the soft organs—lungs, stomach, liver, and intestines—were removed from the body and separately dried in order to reduce the risk of the body decomposing. The earliest evidence for this practice was found in the tomb of Queen Hetepheres I, mother of King Khufu in Dynasty 4.[1] Her organs were wrapped in linen packages and placed in an alabaster canopic chest. Some of the earliest canopic jars were found in the tomb of Meresankh III, who died in Dynasty 4 during the reign of King Menkaure.[2]

This set of canopic jars was found in the burial chamber of a tomb whose owner is unknown (see photo below).[3] The round lids have flat tops and tapering sides that fit flush into the mouth of the jar. The thick-walled jars are only hollowed out to two-thirds of their depth and their uninscribed surfaces have been lightly sanded. From the same chamber, a cylinder seal of black mud with the impression of one of the royal names of King Nyuserre helped George Reisner date the tomb to the 5th Dynasty. JLH

1. Reisner 1942, 155. See also catalogue numbers 1 and 2 for a suite of furniture and inlays from the same tomb.

2. Brovarski 1978, introduction. Meresankh's canopic jars are in the collection of the Museum of Fine Arts, Boston (MFA 27.1551.1–4); see Dunham and Simpson 1974, 8–9 (page 23 incorrectly claims that they are in Cairo).

3. Porter and Moss 1974, 192; Reisner 1942, 311.

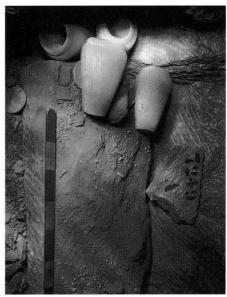

## 34 | MODEL OFFERINGS

a. Duck
Dynasty 5, reign of Djedkare Isesi,
2415–2371 B.C.
Giza, tomb G 4733 E
Egyptian alabaster
H. 4.3 cm, w. 5.1 cm, d. 7.8 cm
Harvard University-Museum of Fine Arts
Expedition 21.2817

b. Bread loaf
Dynasty 5, reign of Djedkare Isesi,
2415–2371 B.C.
Giza, tomb G 4733 E
Egyptian alabaster
H. 3.2 cm, diam. 2.5 cm
Harvard University-Museum of Fine Arts
Expedition 21.2832

c. Joint of meat
Dynasty 5, reign of Djedkare Isesi,
2415–2371 B.C.
Giza, tomb G 4733 E
Egyptian alabaster
H. 4.7 cm, w. 3.0 cm, d. 7.0 cm
Harvard University-Museum of Fine Arts
Expedition 21.2824

d. Fruit or vegetable
Dynasty 5, reign of Djedkare Isesi,
2415–2371 B.C.
Giza, tomb G 4733 E
Egyptian alabaster
H. 1.0 cm, w. 2.1 cm, d. 6.0 cm
Harvard University-Museum of Fine Arts
Expedition 21.2833

Small models representing various foods were
sometimes included in burials as magical substitutes to be consumed in the afterlife. This
grouping, which includes a duck, a conical
bread loaf, a joint of beef, and an unidentified
fruit or vegetable, was once part of a large
assemblage of miniature offerings placed in a
tomb in Giza's Western Cemetery.[1] Although the
owner's name is unknown, a mud seal impression found in the debris of the tomb bears the
cartouche of Djedkare Isesi, a late Dynasty 5
ruler.[2]

Small models of food were merely one means
by which the deceased insured continued sustenance should mortuary priests and descendents
fail to provide essential goods. Another method
was a list of offerings carved into the tomb wall,
often accompanied by an image of the deceased
seated before a funerary meal.[3] In addition to
naming specific foods, the list would include
items such as water, incense, and sacred oils. An
alabaster tablet divided into seven sections with
depressions for ritual oils was also found in this
burial. YJM

1. Reisner recovered ninety-five alabaster models of
food in this burial. Reisner n.d. f, 623–26. See also
Porter and Moss 1974, 136; Brovarski 1988b, 93.

2. Reisner and Smith 1955, 53, fig. 57.

3. For a detailed discussion of offering lists, see Barta
1963.

## 35 | MODEL STONE VESSELS

a. Opening of the Mouth cup
Dynasty 5, 2500–2350 B.C.
Giza, debris of pit G 2347 X
Quartz crystal
H. 3.5 cm, diam. 3.5 cm
Harvard University-Museum of Fine Arts
Expedition 33.1019

b. Model jar with handle
Dynasty 5, 2500–2350 B.C.
Giza, tomb G 2360 A
Egyptian alabaster
H. 8.8 cm, diam. 7.0 cm
Harvard University-Museum of Fine Arts
Expedition 13.3128

c. Model cylinder jar
Dynasty 5, 2500–2350 B.C.
Giza, debris of pit G 7550 B
Egyptian alabaster
H. 5.3 cm, diam. 2.7 cm
Harvard University-Museum of Fine Arts
Expedition 28.1149

d. Model round-bottomed dish
Dynasty 5, 2500–2350 B.C.
Giza, tomb G 4610 A
Egyptian alabaster
H. 2.0 cm, diam. 4.2 cm
Harvard University-Museum of Fine Arts
Expedition 35.2030

e. Model bowl
Dynasty 5, 2500–2350 B.C.
Giza, floor of pit G 7740 Z
Egyptian alabaster
H. 3.7 cm, diam. 4.5 cm
Harvard University-Museum of Fine Arts
Expedition 27.1552

Model vessel offerings were not completely hollowed out because they were intended as symbolic representations rather than as true containers for food and drink. Most are solid with only a slight depression at the top. Even the handle on the small jug of this grouping was suggested rather than fully carved (cat. no. 35b). Nonetheless, such models of eternal stone were highly prized items for both tombs and temples, wherever offerings were made.

Some model vessels had specific ritual purposes. For example, the rock crystal cup here (cat. no. 35a) would have been employed as part of an Opening of the Mouth ceremony.[1] However, most model vessels simply served as miniature substitutes for food, drink, or precious substances, and each one can be matched to an item requested on offering lists. Tall containers, for example, represented liquid offerings such as wine, beer, or sacred oils. The alabaster cylinder jar here (cat. no. 35c) represented a large container of unguent. Cups and dishes represented all types of solid food, and sometimes the actual food was sculpted in stone as well (cat. no. 34). The number of models placed in a tomb's offering area varied widely, from a few to over six hundred in one Giza tomb.[2] JLH

1. Aston 1994, 65, 170, pl. 15a.
2. Junker 1929, 108–9.

## 36 ORNAMENTS FROM A CHAIR IN THE FORM OF "GIRDLE KNOTS"

Dynasty 5, 2500–2350 B.C.
Giza, tomb G 7690 B
Probably bone
H. 20.2 cm, W. 23.3 cm
Harvard University–Museum of Fine Arts
Expedition 29.2217.1–12

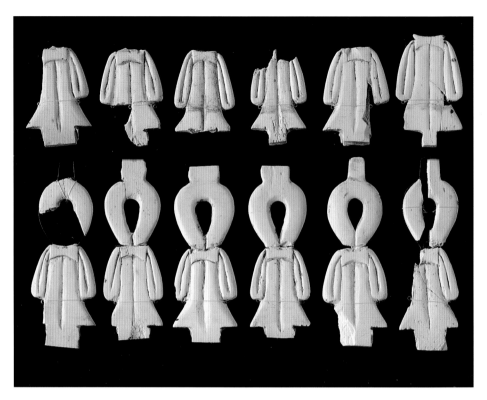

Surviving objects and depictions on tomb walls suggest that beds, chairs, stools, and boxes for storage were popular throughout the course of Egyptian history among those who could afford such luxuries.[1] During the Pyramid Age, furniture was made in a bold, massive, and technically sophisticated style that reflected the accomplishments and restrained elegance characteristic of the period as a whole.[2] A 5th Dynasty representation in the tomb of Seshemnefer, for example, shows the owner seated in a high-back chair with a side panel decorated with three rows of cut-out "girdle knots."[3] The "girdle knot," also known as a "girdle tie" or "Isis knot," is believed to represent folded cloth, perhaps material associated with menstruation and female reproductive powers. The earliest known "girdle knot," from an Early Dynastic burial at Naga ed-Deir, is a gold ornament believed to have served an apotropaic function.[4] Fourth Dynasty chairs featuring openwork designs made of other protective symbols are also known; for example, each side panel of a chair from the tomb of Queen Hetepheres I incorporates an image of a winged falcon on a column (see illustration at right).[5]

The materials used for such furniture ornamentation were often precious. They included gold, silver, semiprecious stones, and ivory. Sources of ivory in ancient Egypt included both elephant and hippopotamus tusk. While the Asian elephant (*Elephas maximus*) supplied some of the ivory during dynastic times, it was the dentine of the African elephant (*Loxodonta africana*) from the Sudanese savanna and the Nilotic hippopotamus (*Hippopotamus amphibius*) that was most commonly used in the fabrication of luxury goods.[6] YJM

1. The stool was the most common type of seating; chairs were a luxury item. See Manuelian 1982, 64.

2. Baker 1966, 39–41.

3. Smith 1946, 291, fig. 141.

4. From Naga ed-Deir N 1532; see Reisner 1908, 29–33, pl. 9. For an example of ornamental "girdle ties" used on a wooden chest from the 3rd Dynasty tomb of Hesire, see Quibell 1913, pl. 18.

5. This chair has not yet been reconstructed. For a reconstruction drawing, see Reisner 1955, fig. 32. For other furniture from the tomb, see catalogue number 1.

6. Krzyszkowska and Morkot 2000, 320–24.

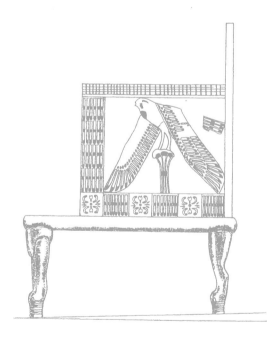

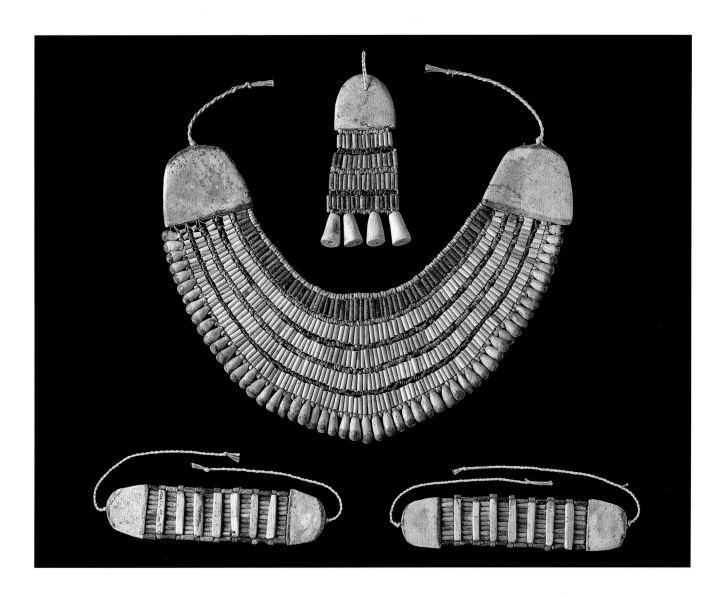

**37 | JEWELRY PARURE**

a. Counterpoise
Dynasty 5, 2500–2350 B.C.
Giza, tomb G 2422 D (with cylinder and
ring beads from tomb G 2416 D III)
Faience
H. 15 cm, w. 3.5 cm, d. 0.4 cm
Harvard University-Museum of Fine Arts
Expedition 37.1312

b. *Wesekh* broadcollar
Dynasty 5, 2500–2350 B.C.
Giza, tomb G 2422 D (with ring beads
from tomb G 2416 D III and tomb
G 1102)
Faience
H. 19 cm, w. 27 cm, d. 0.5 cm
Harvard University-Museum of Fine Arts
Expedition 37.1313

c. Wrist ornaments
Dynasty 5, 2500–2350 B.C.
Giza, tomb G 2422 D (with cylinder beads from
tomb G 2416 D III)
Faience
L. 10.8 cm, h. 5.2 cm, d. 1.2 cm
Harvard University-Museum of Fine Arts
Expedition 37.1311

Much of our knowledge of Old Kingdom ornaments is based on excavated examples from the
Giza necropolis as well as depictions of jewelry
on sculpture and relief. Beaded ornaments
appear to have been popular among both sexes
as well as a range of anthropomorphic deities in
ancient Egypt. Such elaborate adornment served
as colorful additions to the near-white kilt for
men and the plain linen sheath for women.

A recent survey of Old Kingdom broadcollar
representations indicates that there were two
types: the *wesekh* ("the broad one") broadcollar
that consists of multiple, horizontal rows of
densely spaced tubular beads strung in an
upright position, and the *shenu* ("that which
encircles") broadcollar composed of trapezoid-
shaped segments of tubular beads alternately
arranged in horizontal and vertical rows.[1] These
collars were often accompanied by a counterpoise, an element joined to the hemispherical
end pieces at the nape of the neck and hanging
between the shoulder blades. It was designed to
balance the weight of the collar in front and
generally repeated its bead pattern.

Wrist ornaments were particularly favored
by women and often were worn as part of coor-
dinated or matched parures. Wristlets were similar in construction to chokers (cat. no. 18). YJM

1. For a discussion of the various forms of the
collar, see Brovarski 1997, 137–62.

# Dynasty 6

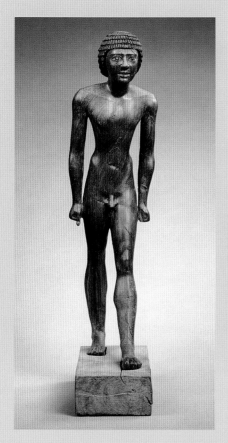

Fig. 38
Wooden figure of Meryrehaishetef,
from Sedment, Dynasty 6, reign of
King Pepy I.

Fig. 39
Relief figure of the overseer of all
works, Nekhebu, Dynasty 6.

The transition to Dynasty 6 was by all accounts uneventful. Iput, wife of the dynasty's first ruler Teti, was probably a daughter of King Unas, the last ruler of Dynasty 5. Additionally, several of Teti's officials, including his vizier Kagemeni, had also served under Unas.[1] Saqqara remained the royal cemetery and kings continued the practice of inscribing magical spells from the Pyramid Texts on the walls of their burial chambers. The texts also appear, in a limited fashion, on the hard-stone sarcophagi reserved for kings. As for the lively scenes of daily life found in 5th Dynasty pyramid temples and causeways, they are no longer as varied or complex. They were transformed into fixed, formalized expressions that define aspects of kingship.

Other trends rooted in the previous dynasty had repercussions that suggest Egypt was experiencing a decline. Several changes, including the increased power of local nomarchs, can be traced to a weakening of the institution of kingship and an ineffective central administration. The nomarchs of Elephantine, for example, controlled access to the granite quarries at Aswan, the prime source of the prized building material, while Pepy I tried to remedy his own decline by marrying two daughters from a powerful provincial family at Abydos, an Upper Egyptian site of growing political influence.

Eventually, Egypt's foreign relationships were affected. For example, the lucrative caravan trade with Nubia came under the control of southern governors. In addition, two relief scenes from private chapels suggest hostile encounters with Libya and western Asia,[2] and a biographical inscription from the Abydos tomb of Weni, a senior official who served Teti, Pepi I, and Merenre, provides the first description of a battle—a land and sea operation near the Sinai region.[3] There are also hints of conspiracies and the usurpation of royal prerogatives. Djau, son of the provincial nomarch Khui and a vizier under Pepy II, was the first non-royal person to place a statue of himself in a temple.[4] The king himself appears to have taken on a more deferential role toward the gods, perhaps a sign of his diminished status during this period.[5]

As in earlier times, royal representation set the standard followed by courtiers and officials. A new style in sculpture[6] and relief characterized by large heads, exaggerated body proportions, narrow waists, undeveloped musculature, elongated limbs, and asymmetry, appeared first in royal art of the 6th Dynasty. The effect is otherworldly—more mystical and transcendent than naturalistic. In private statuary, it is perhaps best reflected in the wooden figures found in serdabs (fig. 38). A great many of these were produced in provincial centers and, like their royal counterparts, are smaller in scale than earlier works. There is also a tendency to depict a single individual at various stages of development, from youth to old age, as illustrated in the multiple images of the architect Nekhebu found in the serdab of his tomb at Giza. Relief work from the chapel of the same burial shows the new style as it applies to two-dimensional work (fig. 39).

Perhaps our best insights into the twilight of the Old Kingdom can be found in the writings of Ipuwer. Although produced at a later date, the text describes a state of chaos and distress believed to reflect the social, political, and economic situation at the end of the Pyramid Age. Ipuwer lamented,

> Lo, the face is pale, the bowman
> ready,
> Crime is everywhere, there is no man
> of yesterday
> Lo, the robber...everywhere,
> The servant takes what he finds.
> Lo, Hapy [the Nile god] inundates
> and none plow for him,
> All say, "We don't know what has
> happened in the land."[7]

YJM

1. Strudwick 1985a, 154–55.

2. Smith 1998, 68.

3. Roccati 1986, 851–52. See also Lichtheim 1973, 18–23.

4. Hornung 1999, 38–39; Strudwick 1985a, 302.

5. Examples include a schist statue of Pepi I kneeling (Brooklyn Museum of Art, 39.121) and a schist sculpture of Merenre I as a sphinx offering *nu* pots, small, globular jars for liquid offerings (National Museums of Scotland, Edinburgh, 1984.405).

6. Russmann 1995, 269–79.

7. Lichtheim 1973, 149–63.

## 38 ORNAMENTS FROM THE TOMB OF PTAHSHEPSES IMPY

a. Bracelet
Dynasty 6, reign of Neferkare Pepy II,
2288–2194 B.C.
Giza, tomb G 2381 A
Gold
H. 0.5 cm (band), diam. 6 cm (band), 2.6
cm (disk)
Harvard University-Museum of Fine Arts
Expedition 13.3414

b. *Wesekh* broadcollar
Dynasty 6, reign of Neferkare Pepy II,
2288–2194 B.C.
Giza, tomb G 2381 A
Gold, lapis lazuli, turquoise, carnelian,
glazed steatite
H. 17.4 cm, w. 17.5 cm, d. 2.5 cm
Harvard University-Museum of Fine Arts
Expedition 13.3086

c. String of beads
Dynasty 6, reign of Neferkare Pepy II,
2288–2194 B.C.
Giza, tomb G 2381 A
Gold, turquoise, carnelian, steatite,
faience
L. 103 cm, diam. 0.8 cm (largest bead)
Harvard University-Museum of Fine Arts
Expedition 13.3422

Excavators discovered the intact burial of Ptahshepses Impy in the large Senedjemib family complex of Giza's Western Cemetery, near the northwest corner of Khufu's pyramid.[1] The oldest mastaba in the group belongs to Senedjemib Inti, a vizier and chief architect under Djedkare Isesi of Dynasty 5. Two sons, Senedjemib Mehi and Khnumenti, held similar positions under King Unas and under King Teti, the first ruler of Dynasty 6. Their grandson, Merptahankhmeryre Nekhebu,[2] served Meryre Pepy I. Nekhebu's son, Impy, was the last of four generations to be buried in the family complex.

Following the family tradition, Ptahshepses Impy held important titles and offices including "count, overseer of all works of the king [under Neferkare Pepy II], architect and builder in both houses, overseer of the two workshops," and "chief lector priest."[3] It is also likely that Impy held the post of vizier towards the end of Pepy II's long reign.[4] On the gold, semicircular terminals of the *wesekh* broadcollar (cat. no. 38b) recovered from the tomb, he is identified by chased hieroglyphs as "the overseer of all works, Impy."

The *wesekh* broadcollar was found on the breast of the mummy in a remarkable state of preservation (see photo at right). It is composed of six double rows of turquoise cylinders, eight rows of ball beads fabricated from gold sheet, one bead row of semi-precious stones at the top, and a row of sixty-three buprestid beetle pendants along the bottom edge.[5] The necklace is unique among broadcollars in its use of turquoise, a prized material imported from the Wadi Maghara in southern Sinai.[6] Another special feature of the collar is the inclusion of buprestid beetles, powerful symbols of resurrection associated with the goddess Neith that date at least as far back as the Early Dynastic tombs of Naga ed-Deir.[7] The beetles are also known from several neck ornaments found in the Giza necropolis,[8] from the Saqqara tomb of Queen Input (mother of Pepy I),[9] as well as the bed canopy of Queen Hetepheres I (cat. no. 1a).

Like many of Egypt's elite, Ptahshepses Impy was buried with a number of other ornaments, including two bracelets that were found on the left wrist: a string of beads[10] and a flat gold band (cat. no. 38a). The band is pierced at each rounded end and surmounted by a disk of gold sheet held in place by string. The disk, as well as the gold, had solar, life-giving associations and would have ensured the deceased continued existence after death. Many of the beads on Impy's necklace (cat. no. 38c) also had symbolic value. The blue-green turquoise represented regenerative growth,[11] the red-orange of the carnelian stood for strength and dynamism, while blue reflected the heavens and the life-giving Nile.[12] YJM

1. Porter and Moss 1974, 89–92.

2. For a biographical sketch of Nekhebu, see Dunham 1938a, 1–8, pl. 1; also Brovarski 2001, 33.

3. Impy's name and titles appear on his inscribed cedar coffin now in the collection of the Museum of Fine Arts, Boston (MFA 13.3085); see Brovarski 2001, 34–35.

4. Strudwick 1985a, 96–97; Brovarski 2001, 34–35.

5. For an analysis of gold from this necklace as well as additional samples of Old Kingdom gold from Giza, see Appendix A. For a detailed description of the beadwork, see Markowitz and Shear 2001, 1–4.

6. The most common bead material for surviving collars of the Old Kingdom is faience. The six double rows of beads in Impy's neck ornament formerly thought to be glazed steatite were recently analyzed by Richard Newman, Head of Scientific Research, Department of Conservation and Collections Management, Museum of Fine Arts, Boston. He determined that the beads were turquoise. For information on ancient Egypt's turquoise source see Aston, Harrell, and Shaw 2000, 62–63.

7. Reisner 1908, pls. 6, 9a.

8. George Reisner records three broadcollars with gilt buprestid-beetle pendants from three different tombs (G 2004 A, G 6012 A, and G 2381 A) dated to the 5th and 6th Dynasties. See Reisner n.d. f, 637–39.

9. Firth and Gunn 1926, 6.

10. A 9 cm long string of carnelian and faience barrel beads now in the Museum of Fine Arts, Boston (MFA 13.3415).

11. The steatite barrel and cylinder beads were once covered by a blue-green glaze, but it has largely disappeared.

12. Wilkinson 1994, 106–9.

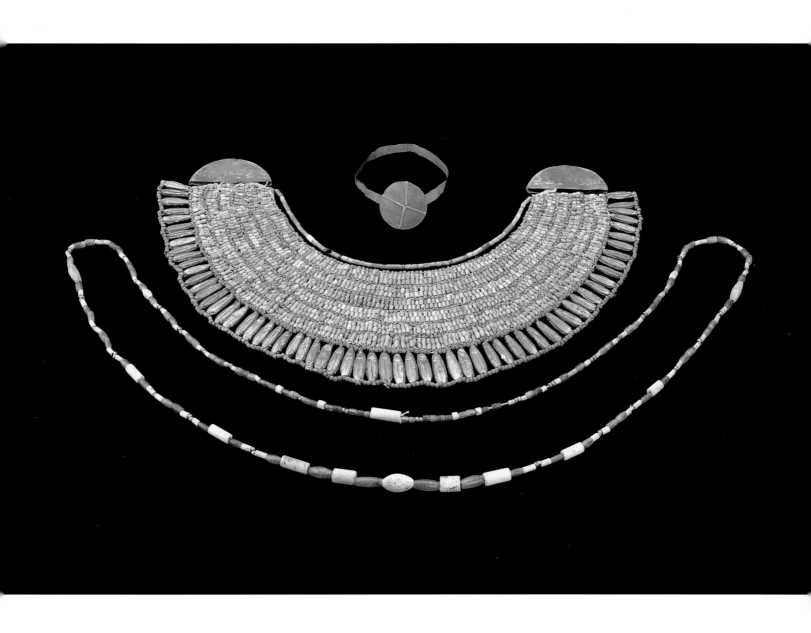

Ornaments on Ptahshepses Impy's body when the coffin was first opened, 1913.

## 39 COPPER MODEL VESSELS FROM THE TOMB OF PTAHSHEPSES IMPY

a. Basin
Dynasty 6, reign of Neferkare Pepy II,
2288–2194 B.C.
Giza, G 2381 A
Copper
H. 2.8 cm, diam. 6.4 cm
Harvard University-Museum of Fine Arts
Expedition 13.2954

b. Neckless jar
Dynasty 6, reign of Neferkare Pepy II,
2288–2194 B.C.
Giza, G 2381 A
Copper
H. 5 cm, diam. 4.2 cm
Harvard University-Museum of Fine Arts
Expedition 13.2957

c. Dish
Dynasty 6, reign of Neferkare Pepy II,
2288–2194 B.C.
Giza, G 2381 A
Copper
H. 1.5 cm, diam. 6.2 cm
Harvard University-Museum of Fine Arts
Expedition 13.3237

d. Offering table
Dynasty 6, reign of Neferkare Pepy II,
2288–2194 B.C.
Giza, G 2381 A
Copper
H. 12 cm, w. 18.7 cm, d. 19.6 cm
Harvard University-Museum of Fine Arts
Expedition 13.2938a–e

e. Spouted bowl with stand
Dynasty 6, reign of Neferkare Pepy II,
2288–2194 B.C.
Giza, G 2381 A
Copper
H. 6 cm, diam.12 cm
Harvard University-Museum of Fine Arts
Expedition 13.2944

Among the burial equipment of Ptahshepses Impy (see also cat. no. 38) were several miniature offering tables and more than a dozen small vessels, all made of copper.[1] These were stored, along with a number of stone vessels and tools, in a wooden box that was placed in front of the deceased's cedar coffin (see photo below).[2] The models, typically deposited in large numbers, would have served the same role as their full-scale counterparts by magically supplying the deceased with food and drink in perpetuity.

An examination of the metal used in the manufacture of the models suggests that the ancient craftsman used a three-step process resulting in copper ingots of high purity (average 99%) with traces of iron, tin, lead, and sulfur.[3] Skilled metalsmiths used the ingots as casting material or cold-hammered the metal into sheets. These shallow vessels were formed by "sinking" the sheet metal into a mold; larger containers were "raised" by hammering the metal against a hard surface and annealing it as needed.[4] Joins, such as those between the sur-face and legs of the offering table (cat. no. 39d), were made by means of copper rivets. A rivet was also used to attach the spouted bowl (cat. no. 39e) to its biconcave stand. YJM

1. Reisner 1913, 59, pl. 15–16.

2. The box had decayed over time so that only fragments remained when Reisner excavated this intact burial.

3. The three steps were smelting, refining to remove slag, and casting in molds. James Muhly of the Department of Conservation and Collections Management, Museum of Fine Arts, Boston, conducted SEM analyses of these vessels in 1979. The trace elements were considered impurities rather than the result of deliberate alloying. See Maddin, Stech, Muhly, and Brovarski 1984, 33–41; Schorsch 1992, 154; Lacovara 1995a, 137.

4. Softening of the metal by heating. Typically, a series of hammering and annealing operations were needed before reaching the final shape. Lucas and Harris 1962, 212–14.

Ptahshepses Impy's burial chamber, 1912.

**40 STONE MODEL VESSELS FROM THE TOMB OF PTAHSHEPSES IMPY**

a. Opening of the Mouth bottle
Dynasty 6, reign of Neferkare Pepy II,
2288–2194 B.C.
Giza, tomb G 2381 A
Quartz crystal
H. 8.4 cm, diam. 4 cm
Harvard University-Museum of Fine Arts
Expedition 13.3268

b. Opening of the Mouth cup
Dynasty 6, reign of Neferkare Pepy II,
2288–2194 B.C.
Giza, tomb G 2381 A
Slate
H. 3.4 cm, diam. 3.5 cm
Harvard University-Museum of Fine Arts
Expedition 13.3258

c. Opening of the Mouth bottle
Dynasty 6, reign of Neferkare Pepy II,
2288–2194 B.C.
Giza, tomb G 2381 A
Slate
H. 7.4 cm, diam. 4 cm
Harvard University-Museum of Fine Arts
Expedition 13.3262

Ptahshepses Impy's wooden sarcophagus was discovered in his intact burial chamber surrounded by an array of funerary objects, including countless small model stone vessels. The shapes of the three illustrated here indicate that they are of the type found in Opening of the Mouth sets typically accompanied by *peseshkef* knives (see cat. no. 17). However, no *peseshkef* knives are listed in the field notes for this tomb.

Because these vessels were not hollowed out—they are solid with only a slight depression at the top—they served a symbolic rather than functional purpose in the Opening of the Mouth ritual. In a complete ritual set there are typically two types of vessels: four cups like catalogue number 40b, and two narrow-necked bottles with flaring rims such as catalogue numbers 40a and 40c. Each vessel type is made half in a dark stone and half in a white stone or crystal.[1] According to the Pyramid Texts, the black and white bottles are lifted up and identified as the black and white eyes of Horus at one point in the ritual.[2] JLII

1. Roth 1992, 115.
2. The ritual is described in Pyramid Text 33. Roth, 1992, 120, 116, notes that written temple inventories provide the ancient Egyptian names for these vessels and tell us that they were made of black and white hard stone. The bottles are called *hatash* and the cups are called *henwt*.

## TOOLS FROM THE TOMB OF PTAHSHEPSES IMPY

a. Model chisel
Dynasty 6, reign of Neferkare Pepy II, 2288–2194
Giza, tomb G 2381 A
Copper
L. 8.9 cm, w. 0.6 cm, d. 0.1 cm
Harvard University-Museum of Fine Arts Expedition 13.3470

b. Round chisel with flat tip
Dynasty 6, reign of Neferkare Pepy II, 2288–2194
Giza, tomb G 2381 A
Copper
L. 8.6 cm, diam. 0.6 cm
Harvard University-Museum of Fine Arts Expedition 13.3468

c. Wide chisel
Dynasty 6, reign of Neferkare Pepy II, 2288–2194
Giza, tomb G 2381 A
Copper
L. 12.8 cm, w. 1.5 cm, d. 0.6 cm
Harvard University-Museum of Fine Arts Expedition 13.3428

d. Mortise chisel
Dynasty 6, reign of Neferkare Pepy II, 2288–2194
Giza, tomb G 2381 A
Copper
L. 12.2 cm, w. 0.7 cm, d. 0.7 cm
Harvard University-Museum of Fine Arts Expedition 13.3426

In a period characterized by monumental building in stone and the widespread sculpting of royal and private statuary, metal tools were of great importance. Because bronze was not available in Egypt until the Middle Kingdom, Old Kingdom stone craftsmen used copper saws, chisels, and drills with an abrasive mix of quartz sand, gypsum, and water.[1] Due to the relative softness of copper, the stone workers would have had to sharpen the tips of their tools repeatedly on slate hones. Leather workers, bead drillers, textile workers, and woodworkers also used copper tools. The last of these used the tools for carving statuary (see illustration below), architectural elements, furniture, ships, and funerary goods.

The chisels recovered from the tomb of Ptahshepses Impy are smaller and lighter in weight than masonry tools and so are either models or sculptor's tools.[2] The tools were made in open-faced or two-part molds while the model was cut from hammered sheet metal. Some items, such as the round chisel with flat tip (cat. no. 41b) and the square-sectioned mortise chisel (cat. no. 41d),[3] would have had wooden handles.[4] Copper chasing and engraving tools, used for making designs and inscriptions on stone and metal, had fine tips and were often hand-held.[5] YJM

1. Lehner 1997, 210–11.
2. Chisels used for cutting or dressing stones are typically 15–20 cm in length; see Arnold 1991, 257–60.
3. For other examples, see Petrie 1917, 19–21, pl. 21.
4. Killen 1980, 16–18.
5. Scheel 1989, 39–40.

## 42 | STATUE OF TJETETY

Late Dynasty 6, 2288–2194 B.C.
Saqqara, near the pyramid of King Teti
Wood
H. 40 cm, w. 10.8 cm, d. 26 cm
Gift of the Service des Antiquités
d'Egypte  24.608

Cecil Firth found a remarkable cache of sculpture in the tomb of Tjetety.[1] One stone and seventeen wooden statuettes of Tjetety, and seven servant figures and funerary models were included in his burial. They were deposited in a recess in the wall of the tomb's shaft.[2] The small serdab chamber protected the sculpture even when the burial chamber itself was completely plundered. Tjetety was a high official; most notably he was "seal bearer of the king of Lower Egypt, overseer of scribes of the sealed documents, and overseer of the double granaries." His tomb has been dated to the time of King Neferkare Pepy II.[3]

In this sculpture overly large eyes angled upwards and long, straight eyebrows lend a quizzical expression to the face. As is the case with much of the sculpture from the end of the Old Kingdom, the head is disproportionately large for the body while the torso is short. The chest and limbs are slender and appear underdeveloped. He wears a short hairstyle with rows of curls on the bottom, topped by striated bangs.[4]
JLH

1. No specific location for the tomb is given; see Porter and Moss 1978, 566.

2. See Peterson 1986, 3, for all the objects from Tjetety's tomb.

3. Strudwick 1985a, 160, no.159 dates the tomb to the end of the reign of Pepy II.

4. This striding wooden figure is carved with extensions on the feet that fit in holes in its wooden base.

## 43 | STATUE OF A SEATED WOMAN

Dynasty 6, 2350–2170 B.C.
Giza, tomb G 1021
Limestone
H. 38 cm, w. 12.5 cm, d. 18 cm
Harvard University-Museum of Fine Arts,
Boston Expedition 21.2603

Originally, cemetery G 1000 in the northwestern part of the Western Cemetery contained a number of burials dating to the end of the 4th Dynasty. As time passed, the spacious, solidly built mastabas of stone were phased out and replaced with smaller ones of poorer quality. George Reisner viewed these additions as a demonstration of the diminished wealth and resources available at the end of the Old Kingdom.[1]

Although the identity of the woman depicted in this statuette is unknown, excavators' comments on the position and architecture of the tomb indicate a 6th Dynasty date.[2] Such a date is confirmed by the lack of naturalism in the figure and the exaggerated body proportions. Notable characteristics of late Old Kingdom art exhibited here include the elongated upper torso, elevated breasts, narrowed waist, suppressed musculature, and long fingers.[3]

The woman is shown seated, wearing a curled wig parted in the center and extending to her broad shoulders.[4] Her face is round, with raised eyebrows, eyelid folds, a long nose, subtle nasolabial creases, a prominent philtrum, and small chin. Traces of red and black pigment on the neck are suggestive of a choker, and wide bands carved at the wrists represent beaded ornaments.[5] YJM

1. Growth in this part of the cemetery was from south to north and from east to west. Many of the later tombs were made of rubble cased with crude brick. For many of these later tombs, the names of the deceased were not recovered. Reisner n.d. f, 1–6.

2. Reisner n.d. f, 1–6.

3. Russmann 1995, 269–79, views this manner of sculptural representation as a "second style" that first appeared in royal statuary during Dynasty 6.

4. The subject sits in an unadorned chair that may have once featured the owner's name.

5. Additionally, there was a considerable amount of black pigment on the hair, in the negative spaces between the arms and torso and between the feet, and on the chair. Traces of black paint also outline the eyes and pupils. Yellow pigment covers large areas of exposed skin. Both arms, including sections of the upper arms, the forearms, and both elbows, have been recently restored. A repair to the right foot and base, made in antiquity, is composed of pink gypsum.

## 44 | FALSE DOOR OF SENWEHEM

Dynasty 6, 2350–2170 B.C.
Giza, tomb G 2132
Limestone
H. 183.2 cm, W. 76.8 cm, D. 24 cm
Harvard University-Museum of Fine Arts
Expedition 27.444

This false door was first photographed *in situ*, in a complete state, by George Reisner's team in 1910 (see inset photo at left).[1] However, when Reisner brought the piece to Boston sometime in 1925, only the top half remained because the lower portion had been stolen.[2] The stolen portion, cut into small blocks, was later found on the Paris art market. The Museum of Fine Arts, Boston, purchased the blocks in 1937 and reassembled the two halves.[3]

The false door belonged to Senwehem, a royal official of Dynasty 6.[4] Senwehem is prominently depicted at the top of the single jambs above four registers of figures on the right and five on the left. Several members of Senwehem's family are depicted in the other scenes. The caption on the drum lintel states: "As for these, they are my children of my body, truly."[5] The oval opening just below the drum at the top of the niche is often referred to as a "serdab squint," as it would have provided a connection into the serdab, or statue chamber.[6]

This false door has a number of unusual features. For example, in the central niche below the drum, Senwehem's son, Weser, embraces a woman named Nefer, likely his mother.[7] One of the earliest hairdressing scenes also appears in the second register down on the right jamb.[8]

JLH

1. See Porter and Moss 1974, 75, for information on the tomb.

2. According to Dunham 1938b, 41, "In 1925 the Expedition found at Giza the upper part of a false-door belonging to a man named Sen-wehem..." No field numbers are given in the field notebook for this object for that year.

3. Capart 1939, 158.

4. His titles were "royal acquaintance, wab priest of the king, and funerary priest." Based on stylistic analysis, Fischer 1976, 50, no. 40, dated the false door to the beginning of Dynasty 6. However, Cherpion 1989, 122–23, presents parallels in iconography to suggest Dynasty 4.

5. Fischer 1976, 50.

6. Brovarski 1988d, 89, notes a serdab in which all the statues faced the serdab squint.

7. The relationship between the figures is not certain, but because of the dominant position of the woman on the spectator's left, Fischer 1959, 248, no. 39, suggests that it must be the mother.

8. Here a small, unnamed hairdresser arranges the hair of the woman named Nefer. See Riefstahl 1956, 16, no. 27; Fischer 1976, 49.

**45 | ARCHITRAVE OF IRYENAKHET**

Dynasty 6, 2350–2170 B.C.
Giza, tomb G 2391 X
Limestone
H. 45.1 cm, w. 185.7 cm, d. 9.5 cm
Harvard University-Museum of Fine Arts
Expedition 13.4333

This large rectangular stone inscribed for Iryenakhet was once an architrave spanning the top of a doorway.[1] It was found in two pieces among the debris of a shaft of his mastaba.[2] Iryenakhet's chief title was "overseer of commissions for the funerary priests of the vizier Senedjemib Mehi."[3] (Senedjemib Mehi had served under Kings Djedkare Isesi and Unas).

Characteristic of Dynasty 6 is the inclusion of several family members on the architrave.[4] The long offering text and the sunken relief decoration are also features associated with this period.[5] While crisp detail is lacking, many small chisel marks inside the sunken relief provide the figures with impressionistic modeling.[6] Iryenakhet and his wife Kaesites stand at the left. Three sons and one daughter bring offerings to them; their names from left to right are Mehi, Senedjemib, Sheshyt, and Khnumenti. The sons are named after the prestigious members of the Senedjemib family under whom Iryenakhet

served in the funerary cult.[7] Across the top of the architrave, an offering prayer to Anubis requests a good burial for Iryenakhet. Five more lines of an offering prayer to Osiris fill the right side of the block. JLH

1. Hölzl 1999, 18, 106, illustrates an architrave of similar size, also in sunken relief, from the cemetery "en echelon" in the Western Cemetery in Giza. It belonged to the 6th Dynasty official Hamekai. It is now object ÄS 8532 in the collection of the Kunsthistorisches Museum, Wien. Also compare ÄS 8524a, b.

2. Porter and Moss 1974, 92. Iryenakhet was one of three generations of priests buried in the tomb complex. The lintels of his son Mehi and his grandson Neferi, both from tomb G 2391, are also in the collection of the Museum of Fine Arts, Boston (MFA 13.4337 and 13.4338).

3. Reisner 1913, 65; Fischer 1968, 222, provides "overseer of the apportionment (of offerings) of (i.e. deriving from) the funerary priests." Jones 2000, 1:96, title no. 400, provides the translation "overseer

of commissions of *ka* priests." He also holds Jones 2000, 1:241, title no. 882, "overseer of the department of tenant-landholders of the Great House."

4. Harpur 1987, 46; she also provides a list of other Giza lintels and architraves with depictions of family groups on page 305.

5. Strudwick 1985a, 24. Sunken relief gained popularity at the end of Dynasty 5 and became the norm for Dynasty 6.

6. Sunken relief is best suited for outside walls, as the sun creates shadows that enhance the carving, and it endures the elements better than the more delicate raised relief.

7. According to Brovarski 2001, 31, note 133, naming children after patrons was often done by late Dynasty 6 funerary priests of the Senedjemib family.

## 46 | HUNTING RELIEF OF QAR AND IDU

Dynasty 6, 2338–2170 B.C.
Giza, tomb G 7101
Painted limestone
H. 53cm, W. 132 cm, d. 14.5 cm
Harvard University-Museum of Fine Arts
Expedition 27.1130

Stela and bust of Idu, tomb of Idu (G 7102), 1925.

The large and spectacular tomb from which this relief came belonged to a Dynasty 6 official named Meryrenefer; he was also known as Qar.[1] Because the "Meryre" portion of the name derived from the prenomen of King Meryre Pepi I, the tomb cannot date before that king's reign (2338–2298 B.C.).

In this scene of Qar hunting, a man named Idu stands behind him. Idu owned a tomb (G 7102) adjacent to Qar's and shared with Qar a number of significant offices relating to the cults of Meryre Pepi I and Khafre.[2] The two were likely father and son, but the texts are not clear as to who was the father and who was the son.[3]

Qar dominates the picture on the right as he hunts birds with his throw stick poised over his head. Idu, depicted on a smaller scale and separated spatially and stylistically from Qar by a vertical line, stands behind him passively holding his throw stick in one hand and three ducks in the other. Both men wear short beards and broad collars. Idu also wears a kilt and bracelets. Their hairstyles are different but both are known from this period: Idu's is long and falls behind his ear

while Qar's is short, curled, and covers his ear. Qar's hair is also bound by a fillet with two papyrus umbrels and one long and one short streamer, common adornments in marsh scenes.

Although Qar's figure is carved higher than Idu's, both men are depicted in low rather than true raised relief. The artist took a shortcut by removing only part of the stone surrounding the figures and then tapering and blending the edges into the background. Other than Qar's eyebrow and cheek area, the figures also exhibit little fine modeling of musculature. The hieroglyphs, especially those around and above Idu, are summarily treated—they are merely incised.[4]

Much of the pigment for the red-brown skin tones and black wigs remains, along with several patches of the gray background color. The red-brown paint was hastily applied, sloshing beyond the figure onto the background. It is apparent that the gray background color was applied after the red-brown flesh color, thereby covering—at least in ancient times— any spills of paint.[5] JLH

1. According to Simpson 1976, 1–2, pl. 4a, and figs. 15, 18, this block was positioned in a stairway that led to an underground chapel in the mastaba. See also Porter and Moss 1974, 184–85.

2. Khentiu-she of the pyramid of Meryre Pepi I and inspector of wab priests of the pyramid of Khafre.

3. Further confusion arises because Qar had a son named Idu and Idu had a son named Qar. Simpson 1976, 1–2, note 2, believes that Idu was the son of Qar, contrary to some scholars. For an overview of the opinions on this relationship and the date of the tomb, see Strudwick 1985a, 69–70.

4. Although it looks as though the incised lines are filled with black pigment, the dark color is encrusted dirt. I would like to thank Susanne Gänsicke and C. Mei-An Tsu, object conservators at the Museum of Fine Arts, Boston, for this information.

5. Again, I would like to thank Susanne Gänsicke and C. Mei-An Tsu for this information. In the throw sticks, hieroglyphs, and other areas, traces of a paler orange paint still remain.

Standing statues in the tomb of Qar (G 7101) with an inscription giving his chief titles, 1925.

## 47 | PLASTER MASK OF NIMAATRE

Dynasty 6, 2350–2170 B.C.
Giza, tomb G 2092 A
Gypsum plaster
H. 22.2 cm, w. 17 cm, d. 20 cm (front to back of head)
Harvard University-Museum of Fine Arts Expedition 37.644

Experiments in mummification during the Old Kingdom were not successful in preserving body tissues, as evidenced by skeletons found inside body-shaped coverings of plaster, mud, or resin-soaked linen.[1] Most of the known body covers of plaster date to Dynasties 5 and 6 and come from upper-class tombs at Giza.[2] George Reisner found this face covering along with several other pieces of thick gypsum plaster and some skeletal remains in a burial shaft belonging to a high palace official named Nimaatre.[3] Together, the fragments once formed a full body cover.[4]

The mask's distinctive facial features—a broad mouth with full lips, deep eye sockets, and clearly defined brow ridges—indicate that it was meant to represent a specific individual.[5] However, because the mask's interior shows only linen fabric impressions and has no facial contours, it is not a true "death mask," a mold made of the face of the deceased. Nevertheless, scholars believe that the mask was made on the face because other known coverings extend well beyond the ears to the back of the head.[6] The thickness of the plaster (up to 3.5 cm in some areas) and the bandaging of the face before the plaster was applied would have prevented the mask from reproducing specific features. Instead, the wet plaster had to be sculpted by hand on the mask's exterior. Both the mask's funerary function and its preservation of an individual's likeness link it to the reserve heads found in other tombs (cat. nos. 9, 10).  JLH

1. David 2000, 373. Renee Friedman of the British Museum recently found non-royal females in a Predynastic burial (about 3600 B.C.) with their heads and hands wrapped in linen. This attempt at mummification dates five hundred years earlier than any previously known examples.

2. Tacke 1996, 321–33, provides twenty-eight examples, all dating from Dynasties 5 and 6. While the majority came from Giza, Tacke also noted three from Abusir and three from Saqqara.

3. "Overseer of palace attendants" was among the lofty titles of this official; for titles and tomb see Roth 1995, 116, and pl. 65b; for the tomb see Porter and Moss 1974, 70.

4. Compare the restored full body cast of MFA 39.828 from nearby Giza tomb 2037 B, illustrated in Brovarski 1988c, 91; see also Roehrig 1999d, 476.

5. A ridge that represents the hairline on this mask is not present on most examples.

6. See Hawass 1992, 336, fig. 6 for a mud and plaster mask that once covered the whole head except for a portion at the back.

## 48 | BEADNET DRESS

Dynasty 6, 2350–2170 B.C.
Giza, tomb G 2342 D
Faience
H. 114.3 cm, W. 73.7 cm (as reconstructed)
Harvard Museum-Museum of Fine Arts
Expedition 33.1020

Although the standard dress for women in ancient Egypt was a plain, linen sheath, depictions of women in sculpture, painting, and relief occasionally feature garments decorated with an overall lozenge pattern.[1] This design is believed to represent beadwork either sewn onto the dress or worked into a separate net that was worn over the linen.

During excavations at Giza, the Boston team found evidence of elaborate beadwork compositions in several tombs dating from the 4th through 6th Dynasties.[2] One intact burial dating to the reign of King Khufu (2585–2560 B.C.) yielded a complete beadnet dress that was later reconstructed with the aid of field notes and photography. Swatches of beads, many with the stringing material preserved, provided information on the arrangement and pattern (see below).[3] A similar beadnet construction made of beads from a 5th Dynasty tomb at Qau in Middle Egypt includes breast caps and a *mitra* shell fringe.[4]

This beadnet reconstruction[5] was made from faience cylinders, floral pendants, and ring beads found in the debris of a subsidiary burial at Giza. Based on the vast number of beads found, the uniform size of the cylinders and ring beads, and the presence of the floral elements, Reisner concluded that these beads once adorned a linen garment.[6] Using the 4th Dynasty beadnet dress from Giza as a model, a form-fitting beaded netting with high waist, halter top, and lozenge-patterned skirt was created. Although the color of the faience beads has faded, the beadnet was originally brilliant blue and blue-green in imitation of lapis lazuli and turquoise. YJM

1. For Old Kingdom examples of women wearing patterned dresses, see Jick 1988, 79, fn. 1.
2. Noel Wheeler cleared the burial in pit G 7440 Z and documented its contents in his April 21, 1927, diary entry. Reisner later described five additional Giza burials (G 7112 A, G 7143 B, G 7765 D, G 4516 C and G 5520), as having faience cylinder and ring beads that "more or less certainly belonged to

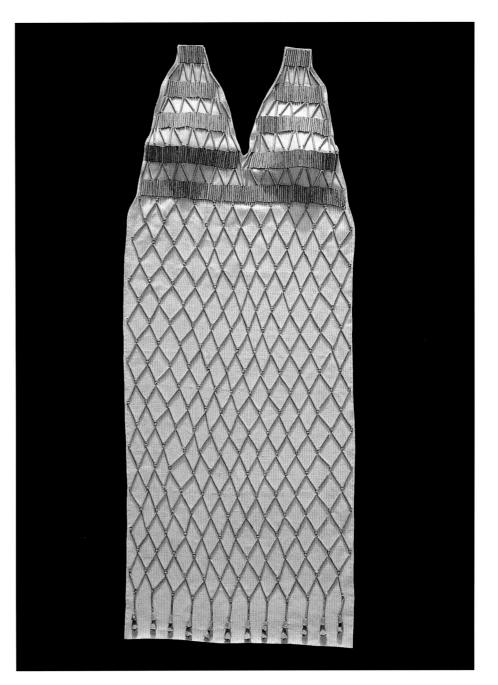

beaded garments." See Reisner, n.d. f, 651–53.
3. The beads from an intact Giza tomb (G 7740 Z) were used to reconstruct another beadnet dress in the Museum of Fine Arts, Boston (27.1548). See Jick 1990, 50–53, and Jick 1996, 73–74.
4. This dress in the Petrie Museum of Egyptian Archaeology, University College London (UC 17743), was restrung in 1994. See Metropolitan Museum of Art 1999, 306–7.
5. Reconstruction of beadwork by Sheila Shear, Consulting Bead Specialist; construction of form by Meredith Montague, Head of Textiles and Costumes Conservation, Museum of Fine Arts, Boston.
6. Reisner n.d. f, 653.

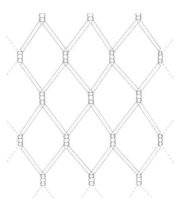

## 49 | STONE VESSELS

a. Jar with pointed bottom
Dynasty 6, 2350–2170 B.C.
Provenance unknown
Egyptian alabaster
H. 17.2 cm, diam. 4.5 cm
Purchased by Albert M. Lythgoe, 1903.
Emily Esther Sears Fund 03.1529

b. Opening of the Mouth cup
Dynasty 6, 2350–2170 B.C.
Sheikh Farag, tomb 5202
Slate
H. 3.8 cm, diam. 3.2 cm
Harvard University-Museum of Fine Arts
Expedition 24.734

c. Cylinder jar
Dynasty 6, 2350–2170 B.C.
Provenance unknown
Anorthosite gneiss
H. 7.9 cm, diam. 5.9 cm
Hay Collection, Gift of C. Granville Way
72.574

The tradition of including stone vessels in the funerary assemblage was maintained throughout the Old Kingdom period. The corpus of vessel types that appeared in Dynasty 4 also continued to be made in the following two dynasties. However, as the Old Kingdom progressed, there was a trend towards having fewer practical vessels in favor of model vessels. Eventually, there was a decrease in the number of model vessels as well.[1]

The cylinder jar of catalogue number 49c was a classic unguent container that was particularly popular in Dynasty 6. The delicate tapering from top to bottom renders an elegant form to this small translucent vessel.[2] Several inscribed examples of this type have been found with the name of either King Pepi I or II, suggesting that they were royal gifts.[3]

The small slate cup of catalogue number 49b is from an Opening of the Mouth ritual set (see cat. nos. 17, 40). The interior was not hollowed out and there is only a slight indentation at the top, so the cup was not meant for practical use as a container.[4] There were usually equal numbers of white (either rock crystal or alabaster) and black (slate) stone vessels in the set. Such cups have also been found on offering tables.[5]

The slender alabaster jar with pointed bot-

tom of catalogue number 49a was likely intended to imitate similarly shaped vessels made of metal.[6] They were also common in both the 5th and 6th Dynasties.[7] JLH

1. Reisner and Smith 1955, 91–92.

2. Aston 1994, 104, no. 35. These containers can range in date from Dynasty 5 to 11.

3. Aston 1994, 104; Ziegler 1999a, 448; Hayes 1953, 127, fig. 77. Reisner and Smith 1955, 93, fig. 137, notes that this vessel type, with small disk lids, was found in the wooden toilet box of Hetepheres containing cosmetics and eye paint.

4. Aston 1994, 140, no. 138.

5. Reisner 1931, 233.

6. Arnold and Pischikova 1999, 122, fig. 72.

7. Aston 1994, 137, no. 127.

## 50 BOWL INSCRIBED FOR KING TETI

Dynasty 6, reign of Teti, 2350–2338 B.C.
Giza, shaft G 2385 A in tomb G 2374
Anorthosite gneiss
H. 4.5 cm, diam. 9.4 cm
Harvard University-Museum of Fine Arts
Expedition 13.3141

This bowl was found in a rubble-filled shaft of the tomb of Vizier Khnumenti, son of Senedjemib Inti. The contents of the shaft had been badly disturbed, but in addition to this object they included a large number of stone food cases (cat. no. 51), bits of wooden statues, a few stone vessels and fragments, beads, and crumpled gold foil.[1]

That this delicate bowl survived at all is miraculous. It is made of anorthosite gneiss, a material composed of translucent white plagioclase and dark hornblend that was used to fashion stone vessels from the Early Dynastic through the Old Kingdom periods.[2] The bowl's finely carved walls are so thin that one can see through them, and the rounded bottom fits perfectly into the palm of one's hand. The carinated or angled shoulder and the recurved rim of this vessel are typical of Dynasty 6 examples.[3]

One of the most interesting features of the bowl is the lightly incised name of King Teti as "king of upper and lower Egypt, the son of Re, Teti, living forever." Khnumenti must have received this treasure as a royal gift from his sovereign.[4] JLH

1. Reisner 1913, p. 58; Reisner and Smith 1955, pl. 45c and fig. 147.

2. Aston 1994, pl. 14b, notes that anorthosite gneiss is often erroneously referred to as diorite.

3. Aston 1994, 85, 134, no. 117; Reisner and Smith 1955, 101; Jéquier 1933, 28–31, fig. 9–13; Jéquier 1934, 107–12, figs. 14, 15, 17, 19.

4. Reisner 1942, 153, 267–68; Brovarski 2001, 30–31, 79, 129, pl. 101b, fig. 94a.

## 51 FOOD CASES

a. Case in the shape of a dressed goose
Dynasty 6, reign of Teti, 2350–2338 B.C.
Giza, tomb G 2385 A
Limestone
H. 25.1 cm, w. 24.5 cm, d. 39 cm
Harvard University-Museum of Fine Arts
Expedition 13.3478–9

b. Case in the shape of a round cake
Dynasty 6, reign of Teti, 2350–2338 B.C.
Giza, tomb G 2385 A
Limestone
H. 9.2 cm, diam. 29.2 cm
Harvard University-Museum of Fine Arts
Expedition 13.3489, 13.3491

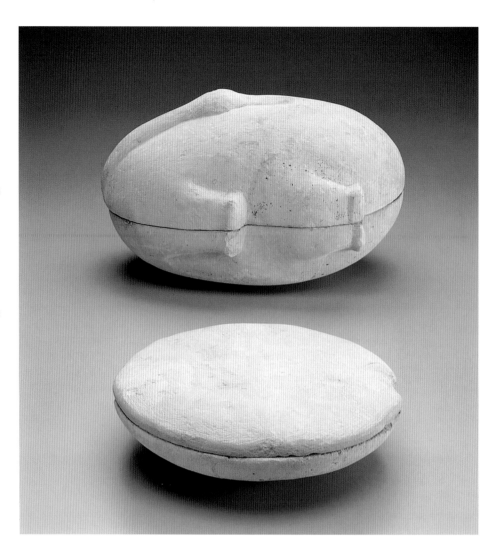

Khnumenti was a son of Senedjemib Inti, a high official who lived during the reign of the late 5th Dynasty ruler Djedkare Isesi. Khnumenti is believed to have served the first 6th Dynasty ruler, King Teti (cat. no. 50). Like his father, Khnumenti held the offices of vizier, chief justice, and overseer of all works of the king,[1] and was buried in the family tomb complex at Giza near the northwest corner of Khufu's pyramid.[2] He was interred in one of the sloping burial passages (G 2385 A) of his stone-built mastaba (G 2374).[3]

When Reisner excavated the Senedjemib complex, he found more than a dozen food cases in the debris of the shaft of Khnumeti's burial. These limestone containers originally contained geese, ducks, small birds, beef parts, cakes, and a variety of breads. Each case consists of an upper and lower half that rests edge to edge with no visible means of fastening.[4] Traces of yellow pigment on both the exterior and interior surfaces suggest that the cases were once brightly painted.

Prepared foods were one means of providing nourishment to the deceased in the afterlife.[5] Offering lists, representations of provisions in relief, and model offerings (cat. no. 34) were all meant to supplement actual offerings left by mortuary priests and relatives. YJM

1. For a list of his titles, see Brovarski 2001, 129.

2. Porter and Moss 1974, 92; Brovarski 2001, 3.

3. Reisner 1942, 153, 267–68; Brovarski 2001, 1–2, 115, 127. Burial passages in Giza mastabas were typically vertical. Khnumenti's was sloped, as was Ptahshepses Impy's (cat. nos. 38–41).

4. It is possible that the halves of each case were secured with strips of linen or thread. See Brovarski 1988a, 93–94.

5. It has been suggested that the use of hard stone for the cases was intentional—if the food offering decayed, the container would magically serve as a substitute. See Hayes 1953, 119.

## 52 | MACE HEADS

a. Mace head inscribed for King Teti
Dynasty 6, reign of Teti, 2350–2338 B.C.
Saqqara
Limestone
H. 6.8 cm, diam. 6.5 cm
Gift of the Service des Antiquités
d'Egypte 24.601

b. Mace head
Dynasty 6, reign of Teti, 2350–2338 B.C.
Saqqara
Wood
H. 6.8 cm, diam. 5.4 cm
Gift of the Service des Antiquités
d'Egypte 24.602

Teti, the first ruler of Dynasty 6, built his pyramid at Saqqara. It was the last royal burial located on a northeast diagonal that includes the 3rd and 5th Dynasty pyramids of Sekhemkhet, Unas, Djoser, and Userkaf.[1] Although the Teti pyramid and its associated structures sustained considerable damage over the centuries, remnants of Pyramid Text decoration survive in the tomb's interior chambers, and a basalt sarcophagus with text was found in the plundered burial chamber.[2] Early excavations of the Teti pyramid complex (conducted by the French) yielded few objects. However, several pear-shaped mace heads inscribed with the king's name were found east of the pyramid.[3]

Stone maces were used in hunting and battle and evolved into emblems of pharaonic power after unification of the north and south (circa 3000 B.C.).[4] Maces are integral to "smiting scenes" in which the king is shown standing with an upraised mace in one hand and the enemy held by the hair with the other—a poignant moment before delivering a lethal blow. Mace handles were made of wood, and inscribed heads of various materials often served as commemorative items.[5]  YJM

1. Siliotti 1997, 116–17.
2. Teti's basalt sarcophagus is the first with an inscription from the Pyramid Texts. See Lehner 1997, 156.
3. Quibell 1909, 72, pl. 5.
4. For information on the different mace forms, see Payne 1993, 148–53.
5. D'Auria 1999, 166–67.

## 53 STRING OF AMULETS

(From left to right)

a. Hand
Dynasty 6, 2350–2170 B.C.
Carnelian
H. 1.9 cm, w. 1.4 cm, d. 0.4 cm
Helen and Alice Colburn Fund  35.1498

b. Sacred eye
Dynasty 6, 2350–2170 B.C.
Carnelian
L. 1.8 cm, w. 1.5 cm, d. 0.4 cm
Helen and Alice Colburn Fund  35.1503

c. Hand
Dynasty 6, 2350–2170 B.C.
Carnelian
H. 1.9 cm, w. 1.6 cm, d. 0.4 cm
Helen and Alice Colburn Fund  35.1499

d. Sacred eye
Dynasty 6, 2350–2170 B.C.
Carnelian
L. 1.8 cm, w. 1.6 cm, d. 0.4 cm
Helen and Alice Colburn Fund  35.1497

e. Human head
Dynasty 6, 2350–2170 B.C.
Carnelian
H. 1.6 cm, w. 1.3 cm, d. 0.4 cm
Helen and Alice Colburn Fund  35.1506

f. Sacred eye
Dynasty 6, 2350–2170 B.C.
Carnelian
L. 1.9 cm, w. 1.6 cm, d. 0.5 cm
Helen and Alice Colburn Fund  35.1496

g. Shell
Dynasty 6, 2350–2170 B.C.
Carnelian
H. 1.7 cm, w. 1.6 cm, d. 0.4 cm
Helen and Alice Colburn Fund  35.1508

h. Sacred eye
Dynasty 6, 2350–2170 B.C.
Carnelian
L. 2.0 cm, w. 1.7 cm, d. 0.5 cm
Helen and Alice Colburn Fund  35.1500

i. Human head
Dynasty 6, 2350–2170 B.C.
Carnelian
H. 1.7 cm, w. 1.4 cm, d. 0.5 cm
Helen and Alice Colburn Fund  35.1507

j. Sacred eye
Dynasty 6, 2350–2170 B.C.
Carnelian
L. 1.8 cm, w. 1.6 cm, d. 0.5 cm
Helen and Alice Colburn Fund  35.1502

k. Human head
Dynasty 6, 2350–2170 B.C.
Carnelian
H. 1.8 cm, w. 1.3 cm, d. 0.4 cm
Helen and Alice Colburn Fund  35.1501

l. Hand
Dynasty 6, 2350–2170 B.C.
Carnelian
H. 1.7 cm, w. 1.3 cm, d. 0.3 cm
Helen and Alice Colburn Fund  35.1505

m. Hand
Dynasty 6, 2350–2170 B.C.
Carnelian
H. 1.7 cm, w. 1.4 cm, d. 0.4 cm
Helen and Alice Colburn Fund  35.1509

n. Hawk
Dynasty 6, 2350–2170 B.C.
Carnelian
H. 1.2 cm, w. 1.8 cm, d. 0.3 cm
Helen and Alice Colburn Fund  35.1504

A popular class of ornament in ancient Egypt was the amulet, a talismanic device whose power depended upon the specific form and material used. Amulets predate recorded history and were worn by adults and children of both sexes. Some of the earliest forms were made of organic materials such as seeds, bone, ivory, and shell. Early representational amulets often took the shape of dangerous animals. They were rendered harmless by the very act of their creation.[1]

While George Reisner recovered a large number of amulets from the late Old Kingdom cemetery at Naga ed-Deir in Upper Egypt,[2] few were found at Giza.[3] Of the twenty-two recorded, none were associated with 4th Dynasty burials—three were dated to late Dynasty 5 and the remainder derived from 6th Dynasty tombs.[4] The dated amulets include the following shapes: hawks, apes, human body parts (heads, arms, hands, fists, and legs), vultures, jackals, lion foreparts, frogs, and sacred eyes.[5]

Late Old Kingdom amulets were made of gold, shell, bone, ivory, steatite, carnelian, green feldspar, calcite, limestone, and faience.[6] Of the hard stones, carnelian was the most popular for human body parts, perhaps because the color is closely related to skin tones. Because carnelian was the hardest stone worked by the Egyptians, it was also a symbol of strength and permanence. The purpose of the body-part amulets was to serve as substitutes should the mummy sustain damage or deterioration.[7]

The three non-human amulet forms incorporated into this string of protective charms are the shell, the hawk, and sacred eye. Representations of the shell (*Cardium edule*) occur in burials beginning in the late Predynastic Period, and although their specific role is unknown, they must have protected the wearer from harm.[8] The hawk is in the archaic crouched position found on the top of *serekh* beads dating to the Early Dynastic Period.[9] It most likely symbolizes Sokar or Horus and would have placed the owner of the amulet under the protection of the deity. The sacred eye (*wadjet*), an emblem of the restored eye of Horus after the god's mythic battle with Seth, had the power to bestow healing and regeneration.  YJM

---

1. The wearer may have also somehow assimilated the power of the evildoer, gaining strength and control over malevolent forces. Andrews 1994, 9, wisely points out that our knowledge of the meaning of these early amulets is speculative.

2. Reisner 1932b, 120–42.

3. Reisner does not include in his corpus of amulets the several dozen beetle pendants found with collars; see Reisner n.d. f, 665.

4. This does not mean that there were no 4th Dynasty amulets, because most of the tombs (and the bodies of their owners) were plundered. Also, Reisner excluded the seventeen amulets, identified as animals, human body parts, and sacred eyes, found in the Menkaure Valley Temple; see Reisner 1931, 235–36.

5. Brunton identified a similar corpus of amulets at Qau. See Brunton 1927, pls. 35–36, 48.

6. Faience, typically glazed a bright blue-green, constitutes more than half of the excavated examples from Giza.

7. For a more detailed discussion of the function of body-part amulets, see Andrews 1994, 69–73.

8. For a list of known contexts, see Petrie 1914, 27, pl. 14; Brunton 1927, pl. 48, no. 56D.3.

9. For an example of this type from the Abydos tomb of King Djer, see Andrews 1981, 40, pl. 18, no. 198. A fine example of a single falcon of gold dated to Dynasty 4 was found at Mostegedda, tomb 312. See Brunton 1937, 94.

## 54 | FLINT TOOLS

a. Double-ended scraper
Dynasty 6, 2350–2170 B.C.
Giza, tomb G 2360 A
Flint
L. 11 cm, w. 2.8 cm, d. 1.5 cm
Harvard University-Museum of Fine Arts
Expedition 13.3452

b. Knife with handle
Dynasty 6, 2350–2170 B.C.
Giza, tomb G 2383
Flint
L. 16 cm, w. 5 cm, d. 0.6 cm
Harvard University-Museum of Fine Arts
Expedition 13.3454

Flint is a microcrystalline form of quartz that occurs as nodules embedded in soft stones such as limestone. It is abundantly available in the Nile Valley and was used by the earliest inhabitants to manufacture simple tools and weapons.[1] Its popularity over the millennia is based on a unique property: when chipped, flint breaks with conchoidal fractures, leaving a sharp cutting edge useful in the home, field, workshop, and construction site. Flint was also crafted into ornaments and vessels, including an inscribed bowl found in the Menkaure Valley Temple.[2]

By the end of the Old Kingdom, flint implements of various shapes were included in burials as part of the funerary tradition (cat. no. 19). Although tools and weapons of flint would continue to be used in daily life, they would rarely demonstrate the skilled craftsmanship characteristic of the late Predynastic and Early Dynastic periods. Eventually, copper replaced flint as the material of choice. Double-ended flint scrapers, for example, were replaced by copper razors of similar shape.[3] YJM

1. Nicholson and Shaw 2000, 29–30. Surface flint, freed from the limestone by weathering, was also plentiful. See Lucas and Harris 1962, 411–12.

2. The bowl was inscribed for the 3rd Dynasty ruler King Hetepsekhemwy. Reisner 1931, 102.

3. Spencer 1980, 92.

## 55 | LETTER TO THE DEAD

Dynasty 6, 2350–2170 B.C.
Naga ed-Deir cemetery N 3500
Papyrus
H. 25.5 cm, w. 15.5 cm
Harvard University-Museum of Fine Arts
Expedition 47.1705

Only fifteen letters to the dead have survived.[1] From their content it is clear that the Egyptians felt they could communicate with the deceased. Those who were in the next world could either help them or curse them here on earth. Maintaining the cult of deceased relatives thus took on great importance.

This letter is composed of black painted hieratic in four vertical columns under a horizontal heading (see line drawing, inset at right).[2] The wear patterns suggest that the papyrus was not rolled but folded, once vertically and once horizontally. The folded letter was then deposited at the tomb.[3] It is addressed to Tetiseneb, the son of a man named Hetepnebi.[4] The letter is unsigned, so the author is not known. Although some passages are difficult to interpret, it is clear is that the letter was written by or on behalf of Tetiseneb's son, who was suffering greatly on earth.[5] The letter asks the deceased to help remove the demons causing Tetiseneb's son his undeserved misery. It ends with a plea: "Heal your child! You must seize this demon...now."[6] JLH

1. Quirke 1988, 106; Grieshammer 1974, 864–70.

2. It is inscribed on the recto of the papyrus (the side with the horizontal fibers uppermost).

3. The tomb from which it came is not specified in the field notes. It is cited only as "N3500, Mizlif's tomb"; see Simpson 1970, 58.

4. Quirke 1988, 106, and Simpson 1970, 58, provide the translation "Tetiseneb." According to Goedicke 1972, 95, however, the name could also be "Pepiseneb." Goedicke also says that the text is addressed solely to Tetiseneb. However, Quirke and Simpson suggest that it is written to two individuals, Hetepnebi and Tetiseneb.

5. See full translations in Goedicke 1972, 95, and Quirke 1988, 106.

6. Quirke 1988, 106.

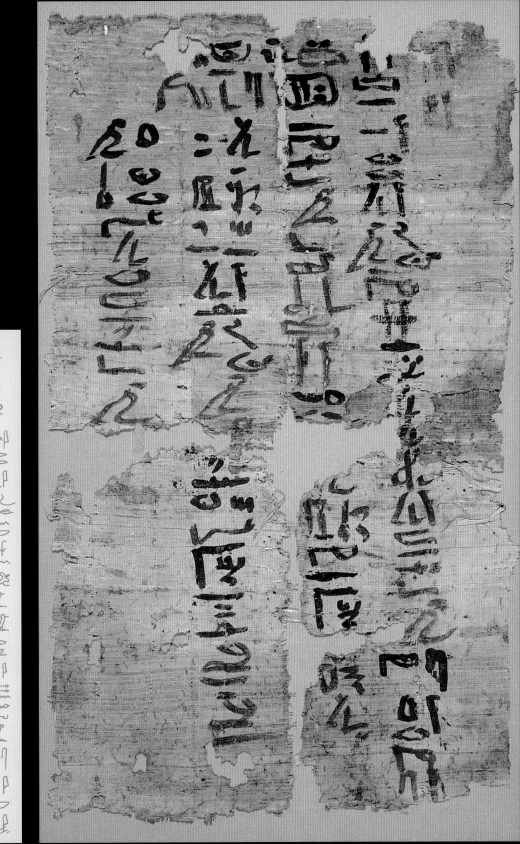

# Appendices

## APPENDIX A
## ANALYSIS OF OLD KINGDOM GOLD ARTIFACTS

Samples from each object (or parts thereof) were taken with a fine scalpel. The small bits of metal, each typically less than one millimeter in size, were then individually mounted in Buehler Epothin epoxy resin and polished so as to reveal a cross-section. The polished samples were coated with carbon and analyzed by wavelength-dispersive X-ray fluorescence in a Cameca MBX electron beam microprobe equipped with a Tracor Northern 5502 energy-dispersive X-ray fluorescence system and a Tracor Northern 1310 stage automation and wavelength-dispersive X-ray fluorescence system (Department of Earth and Planetary Sciences, Harvard University). Three to four areas on each sample were analyzed, using a rastered beam. With one exception, none of the samples appeared to be inhomogeneous when viewed with back-scattered electrons. The exception was the sample from the band of bracelet 13.3414 (cat. no. 38a). The sample contained a substrate metal that had been gilded. The interface between the gilding and substrate showed some diffusion, indicating that the likely method of manufacture was to place a piece of gold leaf onto the substrate and then heat the sandwich.

To produce the quantitative results, pure element standards were utilized, and matrix corrections were carried out on the data by the fundamental parameters (ZAF) method. The ZAF results were then corrected with reference to calibration curves prepared from the analysis of NBS gold-silver and gold-copper microprobe standards. These corrections were carried out by David Lange, supervisor of the microprobe facility at Harvard University.

In the attached table, the average value for each element (and the average analytical total for all three elements) is reported, with the standard deviation given in parentheses.

RICHARD NEWMAN
*Head of Scientific Research*
*Department of Conservation and Collections Management*
*Museum of Fine Arts, Boston*
*December 2000*

**Results of analyses of ancient Egyptian gold by electron beam microprobe**

| Object description and part | Date | MFA # | Wt. % gold* | Wt. % silver* | Wt. % copper* | Total |
|---|---|---|---|---|---|---|
| Cat. no. 38b | | | | | | |
| Foil associated with choker (G 4341 A) | Dynasty 4 | 24.1749 | 69.2 (0.2) | 21.6 (0.4) | 7.4 (0.1) | 98.2 |
| Foil probably associated with broadcollar (G 1360) | Dynasty 5 | 35-8-54 | 49.1 (0.3) | 44.2 (0.5) | 5.7 (0.2) | 99.1 |
| Foil (G 2200 B) | Dynasty 5 | 33-2-115 | 78.0 (0.3) | 17.0 (0.2) | 3.9 (0.2) | 98.8 |
| Foil (G 7143 B) | Dynasty 5 | 27-2-462 | 73.5 (4.3) | 19.9 (3.7) | 5.1 (0.8) | 98.5 |
| Foil associated with rock crystal beetle pendants (G 2360 A) | Dynasty 6 | 13.3424 | 77.0 (0.9) | 17.8 (0.4) | 4.1 (0.2) | 98.8 |
| Cat. no. 38b | | | | | | |
| Broadcollar: bead 10 (G 2381 A) | Dynasty 6 | 13.3086 | 77.5 (0.5) | 16.1 (0.6) | 4.8 (0.6) | 98.3 |
| Broadcollar: bead 25 (G 2381 A) | Dynasty 6 | 13.3086 | 77.4 (0.7) | 16.2 (0.3) | 4.8 (0.4) | 98.4 |
| Broadcollar: bead 37 (G 2381 A) | Dynasty 6 | 13.3086 | 77.7 (0.3) | 16.4 (0.1) | 4.6 (0.1) | 98.7 |
| Broadcollar: end-piece (viewer's right side) (G 2381 A) | Dynasty 6 | 13.3086 | 77.3 (0.6) | 15.6 (0.1) | 4.7 (0.2) | 97.6 |
| Cat. no. 38c | | | | | | |
| String of beads: bead 1 (G 2381 A) | Dynasty 6 | 13.3422 | 73.8 (0.3) | 18.7 (0.3) | 5.4 (0.1) | 97.9 |
| String of beads: bead 2 (G 2381 A) | Dynasty 6 | 13.3422 | 73.9 (1.7) | 17.8 (0.7) | 4.9 (0.1) | 96.5 |
| Cat. no. 38a | | | | | | |
| Bracelet: circular element (G 2381 A) | Dynasty 6 | 13.3414 | 43.0 (0.5) | 29.8 (0.4) | 22.9 (0.2) | 95.7 |
| Bracelet: band (substrate) (G 2381 A) | Dynasty 6 | 13.3414 | 65.3 (0.5) | 22.3 (0.1) | 9.3 (0.1) | 96.9 |
| Bracelet: band (gilt surface) (G 2381 A)** | Dynasty 6 | 13.3414 | 95.8 | 3.0 | 1.1 | 99.9 |

NOTES: *Three to four spots on each sample were analyzed and averaged, unless otherwise noted. The average value for each element is included in the table, with standard deviation given in parentheses. **Only one spot in this area of the sample was analyzed.

## APPENDIX B

### SEAL OF OFFICE

(cat. no. 22)

Dynasty 5, reign of Djedkare Isesi, 2415–2371 B.C.

Reportedly from Northwest Anatolia

Gold

H. 6.4 cm, diam. 2.9 cm

Centennial Gift of Landon T. Clay  68.115

#### Inscription:

The inscription on this seal is composed of two parts: first, the names and titles of the reigning king, Djedkare Isesi (2415–2371 B.C.), and second, the private titles of the seal holder (see illustration at right). The king's Horus name, "Djed-khau," repeated in three *serekhs*, and Horus of Gold name, "Bik-nebew djed," in the top register, indicate that he was the living ruler while this seal of office was in use. The seal also bears a cartouche of King Menkauhor (2425–2415 B.C.), but it is included only as part of a title relating to his pyramid (see title 4 below).

As is customary on cylinder seals of this kind, official titles of private persons appear in the vertical spaces between the repeated Horus names in *serekhs* and in the horizontal band at the bottom. Also, the *serekhs* and the long horizontal text at the bottom face in one direction, while the rest of the vertical inscription faces in the opposite direction. The horizontal text begins at the place where often one should start to read the vertical columns, at the Horus name. The Horus falcons atop the *serekhs* wear more than one type of crown, a common feature of seals with multiple *serekhs* from Dynasty 5 and Dynasty 6.

The four office titles inscribed on the seal are:

1. *Hery-per khentiu-she per-iah*: "chief of the *kentiu-she* of the palace."
2. *Hery seshta:* "master of secrets."
3. *Hem-neter nefer-Djedkare:* "Priest of the pyramid 'Beautiful is Djedkare.'"
4. *Sehedj khentiu-she netery sewt Menkauhor:* "inspector of the *khentiu-she* of the pyramid 'Divine are the places of King Menkauhor.'"

Many scholars have suggested that the first writing of the title *khentiu-she* occurred during the reign of Djedkare. However, all agree that it has a much older oral history originating several reigns earlier. Recently, Ann Macy Roth found a written example that she has dated back further than Djedkare, to Nyuserre (2455–2425 B.C.), based on stylistic evidence. JLH

#### Construction:

This cylinder seal was assembled from four separate pieces of gold—an outer cylinder, an inner cylinder, and two flat rings at the top and bottom. The absence of seams or solder joins on the bodies of both cylinders suggests that these sections were cast using the "lost wax" method. To create hollow parts such as open cylinders or spouts for vessels, a waxy substance would have been applied around a clay or organic core. The surface then would have been coated with clay and the item heated to remove the wax. Finally, molten metal would have been poured into the empty channel and the clay covering and core removed after cooling. Evidence of this technique extends as far back as the Early Dynastic Period and may have been used in the creation of large-scale statuary. It is difficult to determine whether the circular end-pieces were cast or hand-wrought, but the crafting of gold sheet by hammering would have been the simplest method of forming these discs.

The thickness of the metal on the outer cylinder is 0.6 mm and the hieroglyphs that decorate the surface were probably made with a copper chasing tool. The depressed areas, which create an intaglio effect, include outlines made with a single stroke of the chaser as well as furrows formed by multiple strokes. The depth of the grooves varies and it appears as if metal may have been removed in some instances, a result of repeated use of the chaser. Fine detailing and texturing of the surface within the hieroglyphs create a play of light and shadow, features that make this seal a miniature work of art as well as a historical document. YJM

**Material Analysis:**

Non-destructive energy-dispersive X-ray fluorescence conducted by the Scientific Research Laboratory at the Museum of Fine Arts, Boston, indicates that the alloy of this cylinder seal contains gold and silver, with some copper. An analysis of an area on the top where solder appears to be present did not reveal the presence of any elements other than those in the alloy itself.

In order to quantitatively determine the alloy(s) used to make the seal, small solid pieces of metal were cut with a surgical scalpel from edges of losses. These were mounted in Buehler Epothin epoxy resin and polished for analysis in an electron beam microprobe. Three spots were analyzed on each of four samples, which came from three of the four individual pieces of metal from which the seal was made. The results were as follows:

The analyses indicate that the metal used in the cylinder could have been a natural alloy of gold and silver to which copper was added (natural gold or gold-silver alloys usually do not contain much more than about two percent copper). The outer cylinder and top ring are virtually identical in composition, suggesting they may have come from the same batch of metal. The inner cylinder is similar, but appears to contain a little less copper and a little more silver. The ratios of gold to silver in all three areas, however, are virtually identical (a little over 2 to 1), indicating perhaps that all came from one batch of gold-silver alloy.

The cylinder seal is filled with a white to gray material, tinted pale green in places. FTIR analysis of samples showed only calcium carbonate. The outer surface of the seal contains some patches of gray, green, and red materials. The gray deposits are translucent and somewhat hard; FTIR analysis showed that these consist of calcium carbonate (calcite). The green deposits are quite soft and transparent; FTIR indicated the presence of beeswax and the pigment Prussian blue, which was invented about 1700. The presence of this pigment indicates that the deposits are applied and do not represent natural corrosion or accretions from the burial environment. RN & MD

| Element* | Sample 1 outer cylinder | Sample 2 outer cylinder | Sample 3 inside cylinder | Sample 4 top ring |
|---|---|---|---|---|
| Gold (wt.%) | 60.5 (±0.7) | 61.2 (±0.8) | 61.3 (±0.2) | 61.4 (±1.1) |
| Silver (wt.%) | 28.8 (±0.3) | 28.7 (±1.2) | 30.1 (±0.5) | 28.3 (±1.6) |
| Copper (wt.%) | 9.8 (±0.3) | 9.9 (±0.7) | 8.6 (±0.3) | 10.3 (±1.8) |
| Gold/silver | 2.10 | 2.13 | 2.04 | 2.17 |
| Total (wt.%) | 99.1 | 99.8 | 100.0 | 100.0 |

*The weight percentages for each element are averages from three spot analyses with standard deviations given in parentheses.

Line drawing of the inscription on the seal (cat. no. 22).

# Glossary

*Ankh.* Hieroglyphic sign and emblem meaning "life."

**Anubis.** Jackal deity, guardian of the necropolis, and associated with mummification.

**Canopic chest.** Wood or stone chest divided into four compartments used to hold the viscera of a mummified body.

**Cartouche.** Oval that encloses the nomen and prenomen of the king or queen; represents a never-ending loop of rope, knotted at the base.

**Double crown.** King's crown worn to symbolize the unity of the Two Lands. It combined the White Crown of Upper Egypt and the Red Crown of Lower Egypt.

**Faience.** Non-clay ceramic composed of quartz, lime, and alkali. When combined with water, it can be modeled by hand or shaped in a mold. Upon heating, a reflective, vitreous glaze forms on the surface.

**False door.** An imitation stone doorway in a tomb, through which the spirit of the deceased could freely pass to receive offerings and to travel from the tomb to the heavenly realm.

*Heb-sed.* Festival of the renewal of kingship, usually held after thirty years of a king's reign, and thereafter at more frequent intervals; also called the Sed festival.

**Horus.** A son of Osiris and Isis, Horus was awarded the throne of Egypt after a long struggle against Seth, his father's brother and murderer; the embodiment of kingly power shown as a falcon or a man with a falcon's head.

**Horus name.** The first name in the king's titulary, identifying him with the god Horus; written inside a *serekh.*

*Ka.* One of the spiritual components of an individual, symbolized by upraised arms. Sometimes translated as "life force," it was created at a person's birth and survived death, residing in the tomb as a recipient of the offerings left for the deceased.

**Mastaba.** Rectangular stone or mudbrick superstructure of an Old Kingdom tomb whose top is typically flat and walls slanted.

*Nemes.* Headdress worn by kings consisting of a striped headcloth with lappets in front and tied in the back.

**Nomarch.** The highest official in a nome. They were often hereditary rulers. In the late Old Kingdom they began to govern independently from the king.

**Nome.** An administrative province of Egypt.

**Nomen.** The given name of the king, enclosed in a cartouche, accompanied by the epithet "Son of Re."

**Opening of the Mouth.** Ceremony in which priests perform rituals intended to bring the deceased to life in the next world; also performed on statues and images in relief in the tomb.

**Osiris.** God of the underworld, husband of Isis, and father of Horus; transfigured dead king became Osiris during the 5th Dynasty.

**Prenomen.** The religious name of the king given at the time of ascending the throne, accompanied by the epithet "King of Upper and Lower Egypt."

**Portcullis.** Large stone placed in an entranceway to block passage.

**Pseudogroup.** Free-standing statue with multiple images of the same individual.

**Pyramid Texts.** Religious texts carved or painted on the pyramid chamber walls of the 5th and 6th Dynasty rulers.

**Re.** Creator/sun god whose cult was located in Heliopolis; incorporated into the king's titles during Dynasty 4 and manifested by the sun temples of Dynasties 5–6.

**Red Crown.** The crown of Lower Egypt.

**Serdab.** Arabic word for storeroom; the chamber in a tomb in which the statues were stored.

*Serekh.* Image of a palace façade with an open rectangle on top. The Horus name of the king is written in the rectangle, and a falcon, the symbol of Horus, perches on top.

*Shendyt.* The short linen kilt worn by the king.

**Stela.** Inscribed rectangular or rounded slab of stone or sometimes wood; stelae could be carved or painted. They could be found in tombs, serving as funerary monuments. Votive or commemorative stelae were placed in temples.

**Upper and Lower Egypt.** The two traditional geographical divisions of Egypt. Because the Nile flows from south to north, the southern part of the land is called Upper Egypt, while the north, including the Delta, is Lower Egypt.

*Uraeus.* Serpent in the form of a rearing cobra with inflated hood; a symbol of kingship attached to the front of the crown or *nemes.*

**Vizier.** The highest-ranking official in the administration.

**Wab.** Purification priest of lower rank.

**Wadi.** Dry river bed.

*Wesekh* **collar.** Known as "the broad one," it was a popular beaded neck ornament worn by both sexes and a range of anthropomorphic deities.

**White Crown.** Mitre-shaped crown of Upper Egypt.

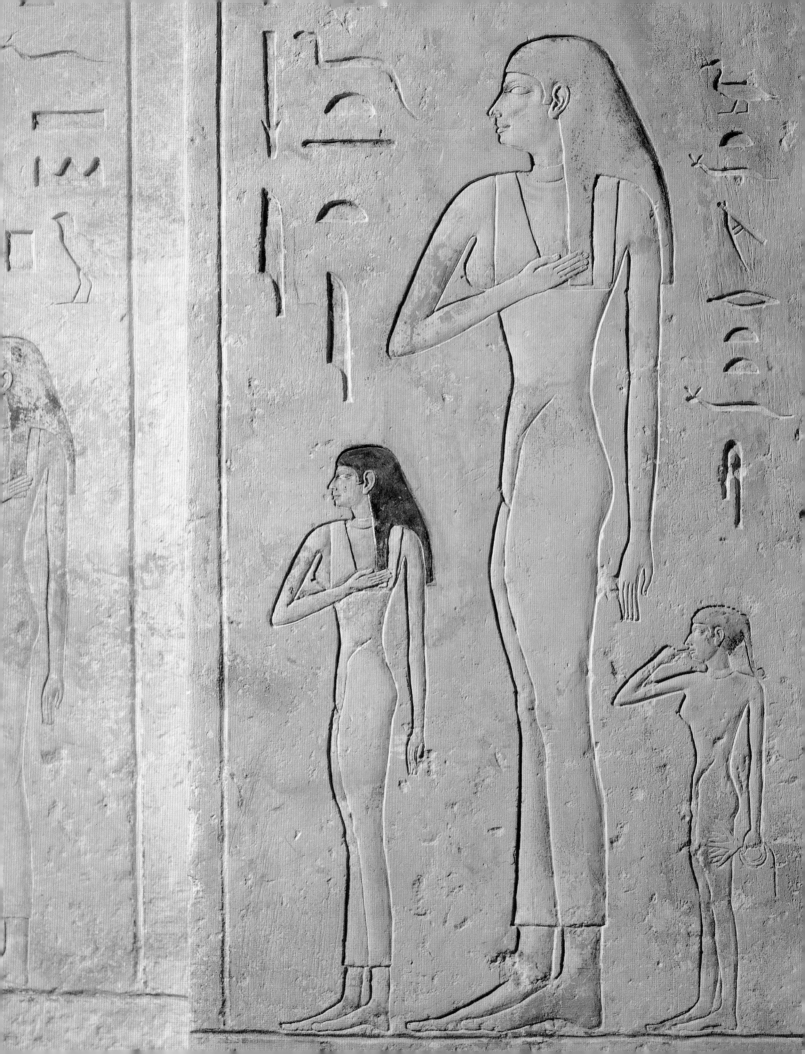

# Bibliography

Abou-Ghazi, Dia'. 1980. *Denkmäler des Alten Reiches III: Alters and Offering Tables.* Fasc. 2, *Nos. 57024–57049* of *Catalogue général des antiquités égyptiennes du Musée du Caire 57001–57100.* Rev. ed. Cairo: Institut français d'archéologie orientale.

Altenmüller, Hartwig. 1998. "Daily Life in Eternity—The Mastabas and Rock-cut Tombs of Officials." *In Egypt: The World of the Pharaohs,* ed. Regine Schulz and Matthias Seidel, 78-93. Cologne: Köln.

Andrassy, P. 1994. "Die hntjwšim Alten Reich." In *Ägyptische Tempel—Struktur, Funktion und Programm / Akten der Ägyptologischen Tempeltagungen in Gosen 1990 und in Mainz 1992.* Hildesheimer ägyptologische Beiträge 37, ed. R. Gundlach and M. Rochholz, 3–12. Hildesheim: Gerstenberg.

Andrews, Carol. 1981. *Jewellery I: From the Earliest Times to the Seventeenth Dynasty.* Vol. 6, *Catalogue of Egyptian Antiquities in the British Museum.* London: British Museum Publications.

———. 1990. *Ancient Egyptian Jewellery.* London: British Museum Publications.

———. 1994. *Amulets of Ancient Egypt.* Austin: University of Texas Press.

Arnold, Dieter. 1991. *Building in Egypt: Pharaonic Stone Masonry.* New York: Oxford University Press.

———. 1994. *Lexikon der ägyptischen Baukunst.* Zurich: Artemis.

———. 1997. "Royal Cult Complexes of Old and Middle Kingdoms." In *Temples of Ancient Egypt,* ed. Byron Shafer, 31–85. Ithaca, N.Y.: Cornell University Press.

———. 1999. "Old Kingdom Statues in Their Architectural Setting." In *Egyptian Art in the Age of the Pyramids,* 41–49. Exh. cat. New York: Metropolitan Museum of Art.

Arnold, Dorothea. 1999. *When the Pyramids Were Built: Egyptian Art of the Old Kingdom.* New York: Rizzoli International Publications.

Arnold, Dorothea, and Janine Bourriau, eds. 1993. *An Introduction to Ancient Egyptian Pottery: Techniques and Traditions of Manufacture in the Pottery of Ancient Egypt.* Mainz am Rhein: Philipp von Zabern.

Arnold, Dorothea, and Elena Pischikova. 1999. "Stone Vessels." In *Egyptian Art in the Age of the Pyramids,* 121–31. Exh. cat. New York: Metropolitan Museum of Art.

Aston, Barbara G. 1994. *Ancient Egyptian Stone Vessels: Materials and Forms.* Studien zur Archäologie und Geschichte Altägyptens 5. Heidelberg: Heidelberg Orientverlag.

Aston, Barbara, James Harrell, and Ian Shaw. 2000. "Stone." In *Ancient Egyptian Materials and Technology,* ed. Paul Nicholson and Ian Shaw, 5–77. Cambridge: Cambridge University Press.

Baer, Klaus. 1960. *Rank and Title in the Old Kingdom.* Chicago: University of Chicago Press.

Baker, Hollis S. 1966. *Furniture in the Ancient World: Origins and Evolution, 3100–475 B.C.* London: Macmillan.

Barta, Winfried. 1963. *Die altägyptische Opferliste von der Frühzeit bis zur griechisch-römischen Epoche.* Münchener ägyptologische Studien 3. Berlin: B. Hessling.

Baud, Michel. 1996. "La Date d'apparition des Hntywš." *Bulletin de l'Institut français d'archéologie orientale* 96:13–50.

———. 1999. *Famille royale et pouvoir sous l'Ancien Empire égyptien.* 2 vols. Cairo: Institut français d'archéologie orientale.

Beckerath, Jürgen von. 1999. *Handbuch der ägyptischen Königsnamen.* Mainz: Verlag Philipp Von Zabern.

Begelsbacher-Fischer, Barbara L. 1981. *Untersuchungen zur Götterwelt des Alten Reiches im Spiegel der Privatgräber der IV und V Dynastie.* Orbis biblicus et orientalis 37. Freiburg: Universitätverlag; Göttingen: Vandenhoeck and Ruprecht.

Bolshakov, Andrey O. 1992. "Princess H.M.T.-Rc(w): The First Mention of Osiris?" *Chronique d'Égypte* 67:203–10.

Borchardt, Ludwig. 1913. *Das Grabdenkmal des Königs Sáhu-re' Band II: Die Wandbilder.* Leipzig: J. C. Hinrichs.

Breasted, James Henry, Jr. 1906. *Ancient Records of Egypt I.* Chicago: University of Chicago Press.

———. 1948. *Egyptian Servant Statues.* Bollingen Series 13. New York: Pantheon Books.

Brewer, D., and E. Teeter. 1999. *Egypt and the Egyptians.* Cambridge: Cambridge University Press.

Brovarski, Edward. 1978. *Canopic Jars.* Corpus Antiquitatum Aegyptiacarum, Museum of Fine Arts, Boston, Fascicle 1. Mainz am Rhein: Philipp von Zabern.

———. 1988a. "Food Cases." In *Mummies and Magic: The Funerary Arts of Ancient Egypt,* ed. Sue D'Auria, Peter Lacovara, and Catharine H. Roehrig, 93–94. Exh. cat. Boston: Museum of Fine Arts, Boston.

———. 1988b. "Model Offerings." In *Mummies and Magic: The Funerary Arts of Ancient Egypt,* ed. Sue D'Auria, Peter Lacovara, and Catharine H. Roehrig, 93. Exh. cat. Boston: Museum of Fine Arts, Boston.

————. 1988c. "Mummy Covering." In *Mummies and Magic: The Funerary Arts of Ancient Egypt*, ed. Sue D'Auria, Peter Lacovara, and Catharine H. Roehrig, 91–92. Exh. cat. Boston: Museum of Fine Arts, Boston.

————. 1988d. "Serdab Group." In *Mummies and Magic: The Funerary Arts of Ancient Egypt*, ed. Sue D'Auria, Peter Lacovara, and Catharine H. Roehrig, 88–89. Exh. cat. Boston: Museum of Fine Arts, Boston.

————. 1991. "Naga ed-Deir." Ph.D. diss., University of Chicago.

————. 1997. "Old Kingdom Beaded Collars." In *Ancient Egypt, the Aegean and the Near East: Studies in Honour of Martha Rhoads Bell*, ed. Jacke Phillips, 137–62. San Antonio: Van Siclen.

————. 2001. *The Senedjemib Complex Part I: The Mastabas of Senedjemib Inti (G 2370), Khnumente (G 2374), and Senedjemib Mehi (G 2378)*. Giza Mastabas Series 7. Boston: Museum of Fine Arts, Boston.

Brunton, Guy. 1927. *Qau and Badari*. Vol. 1. London: British School of Archaeology in Egypt.

————. 1937. *British Museum Expedition to Middle Egypt, First and Second Years, 1928, 1929: Mostagedda and the Tasian Culture*. London: B. Quaritch.

Capart, Jean. 1939. "Une stèle d'Ancien Empire complétée." *Chronique d'Égypte* 14:158.

Capel, Anne K. 1996. "Pair Statue of Queen Hetepheres II and Her Daughter Meresankh III." In Mistress of the House, Mistress of Heaven, ed. Anne K. Capel and Glenn Markoe, 103–4. Cincinnati: Hudson Hills Press.

Cherpion, Nadine. 1989. *Mastabas et hypogées d'Ancien Empire: la problème de la datation*. Brussels: Connaissance de l'Égypte ancienne.

————. 1998. "La Statuaire privée d'Ancien Empire: indices de datation." In *Les Critères de datation stylistiques à l'Ancien Empire*, ed. Nicolas Grimal, 97–142. Cairo: Institut français d'archéologie orientale.

Curto, Silvio. 1963. *Gli scavi italiani a el-Ghiza*. Rome: Centro per la antichità e la storia dell'arte Vicino Oriente.

D'Auria, Sue. 1999. "Mace Heads." In *Art of the Ancient Mediterranean World*, 166–67. Exh. cat. Nagoya, Japan: Nagoya/Museum of Fine Arts, Boston.

D'Auria, Sue, Peter Lacovara, and Catharine H. Roehrig. 1988. *Mummies and Magic: The Funerary Arts of Ancient Egypt*. Exh. cat. Boston: Museum of Fine Arts, Boston.

David, Rosalie. 2000. "Mummification." In *Ancient Egyptian Materials and Technology*, ed. Paul Nicholson and Ian Shaw, 372–89. Cambridge: Cambridge University Press.

Dunham, Dows. 1938a. "The Biographical Inscriptions of Nekhebu in Boston and Cairo." *Journal of Egyptian Archaeology* 24:1–8.

————. 1938b. "Department of Egyptian Art." *Sixty-third Annual Report* (Museum of Fine Arts, Boston):40–43.

————. 1958. *The Egyptian Department and Its Excavations*. Boston: Museum of Fine Arts, Boston.

————. 1978. *Zawiyet el-Aryan: The Cemeteries Adjacent to the Layer Pyramid*. Boston: Museum of Fine Arts, Boston.

Dunham, Dows, and William Kelly Simpson. 1974. *The Mastaba of Queen Mersyankh III, G 7530–7540*. Giza Mastabas Series 1. Boston: Museum of Fine Arts, Boston.

Eaton-Krauss, Marianne. 1995. "Pseudo-Groups." In *Kunst des Alten Reiches: Symposium im Deutschen Archäologischen Institut Kairo am 29. und 30. Oktober 1991*, 57–74. Sonderschrift des Deutsches Archäologisches Instituts Abteilung Kairo 28. Mainz: Philipp von Zabern.

Edwards, I. E. S. 1985. *The Pyramids of Egypt*. Rev. ed. Harmondsworth, Middlesex: Penguin Books.

Épron, Lucienne, and François Daumas, illustrators. 1939. *Le Tombeau de Ti*. Cairo: Institut français d'archéologie orientale.

Faulkner, Raymond. 1962. *A Concise Dictionary of Middle Egyptian*. Oxford: Griffith Institute.

Fay, Biri. 1998. "Royal Women as Represented in Sculpture during the Old Kingdom." In *Les Critères de datation stylistique à l'Ancien Empire*, ed. Nicolas Grimal, 159–86. Cairo: Institut français d'archéologie orientale.

Firth, Cecil M., and Battiscombe Gunn. 1926. *Excavations at Saqqara: Teti Pyramid Cemeteries*. 2 vols. Cairo: Institut français d'archéologie orientale.

Fischer, Henry G. 1959. "A Scribe of the Army in a Saqqara Mastaba of the Early Fifth Dynasty." *Journal of Near Eastern Studies* 18:233–72.

————. 1968. *Dendera in the Third Millenium B.C. down to the Theban Domination of Upper Egypt*. Locust Valley, N.Y.: J. J. Augustin.

————. 1976. *Varia*. Egyptian Studies 1. New York: Metropolitan Museum of Art.

————. 1978. "Five Inscriptions of the Old Kingdom." *Zeitschrift für ägyptische Sprache und Altertumskunde* 105:42–59.

Friedman, Florence Dunn. 1998. "Faience: The Brilliance of Eternity." In *Gifts of the Nile: Ancient Egyptian Faience*, 15–21. Exh. cat. London: Thames and Hudson in association with the Museum of Art, Rhode Island School of Design.

Gardiner, Sir Alan. 1982. *Egyptian Grammar: Being an Introduction to Hieroglyphs*. 3rd ed. Reprint. Oxford: Griffith Institute.

Goedicke, Hans. 1967. *Königliche Dokumente aus dem alten Reich*. Wiesbaden: Otto Harrassowitz.

————. 1972. "The Letter to the Dead, Nag' ed-Deir N 3500." *Journal of Egyptian Archaeology* 58:95–98.

Grieshammer, Richard. 1974. "Briefe an Tote." *Lexikon der Ägyptologie* l, cols. 864–70. Weisbaden: Otto Harrassowitz.

Grimal, Nicholas. 1992. *A History of Ancient Egypt*. Translated by Ian Shaw. Cambridge: Blackwell.

Harpur, Yvonne. 1987. *Decoration in Egyptian Tombs of the Old Kingdom: Studies in Orientation and Scene Content*. London and New York: Kegan Paul International.

Hassan, Selim. 1932. *Excavations at Giza.* Vol. 1, 1929–1930. Oxford: Faculty of Arts of the Egyptian University with the collaboration of Foad Boghdady.

———. 1953. *Excavations at Giza.* Vol. 7, 1935–1936: *The Mastabas of the Seventh Season and Their Description.* Cairo: Faculty of Arts of the Egyptian University.

Hawass, Zahi. 1992. "A Burial with an Unusual Plaster Mask in the Western Cemetery of Khufu's Pyramid." In *The Followers of Horus. Studies Dedicated to Michael Allen Hoffman,* ed. Renée Friedman and Barbara Adams, 327–36. Egyptian Studies Association Publication No. 2 Oxbow Monograph 20. Oxford: Oxbow Books.

———. 1995a. "A Group of Unique Statues Discovered at Giza I: Statues of the Overseers of the Pyramid Builders." In *Kunst des Alten Reiches: Symposium im Deutschen Archäologischen Institut Kairo am 29. und 30. Oktober 1991,* 91–95, pls. 31–32. Sonderschrift des Deutsches Archäologisches Instituts Abteilung Kairo 28. Mainz: Philipp von Zabern.

———. 1995b. "A Group of Unique Statues Discovered at Giza II: An Unfinished Reserve Head and a Statuette of an Overseer." In *Kunst des Alten Reiches: Symposium im Deutschen Archäologischen Institut Kairo am 29. und 30. Oktober 1991,* 97–101, pls. 33–35. Sonderschrift des Deutsches Archäologisches Instituts Abteilung Kairo 28. Mainz: Philipp von Zabern.

Hayes, William C. 1953. *The Scepter of Egypt I: From the Earliest Times to the End of the Middle Kingdom.* New York: Metropolitan Museum of Art.

Hölzl, Regina. 1999. *Reliefs und Inschriftensteine des Alten Reiches I.* Corpus Antiquitatum Aegyptiacarum, Kunsthistorisches Museum Wien, Lfg. 18. Mainz am Rhein: Philipp von Zabern.

Hornung, Erik. 1999. *History of Ancient Egypt: An Introduction.* Ithaca, N.Y.: Cornell University Press.

Houlihan, Patrick F. 1986. *The Birds of Ancient Egypt.* Warminster: Aris and Phillips.

Jacquet-Gordon, Helen K. 1962. *Les Noms des domaines funéraires sous l'Ancien Empire.* Institut français d'archéologie orientale bibliothèque d'étude 34. Cairo: Institut français d'archéologie orientale.

Jánosi, Peter. 1999. "The Tombs of Officials: Houses of Eternity." In *Egyptian Art in the Age of the Pyramids,* 27–39. Exh. cat. New York: Metropolitan Museum of Art.

Jéquier, Gustave. 1933. *Fouilles à Saqqarah: Les Pyramides des reines Neit et Apouit.* Cairo: Institut français d'archéologie orientale.

———. 1934. "Vases de pierre de la VIème dynastie." *Annales du services des antiquités de l'Égypte* 34:97–113.

Jick, Millicent. 1988. "Bead-Net Dress." In *Mummies and Magic: The Funerary Arts of Ancient Egypt,* ed. Sue D'Auria, Peter Lacovara, and Catharine H. Roehrig, 78–79. Exh. cat. Boston: Museum of Fine Arts, Boston.

———. 1990. "Bead-net Dress from Giza Tomb G7740Z Old Kingdom Dynasty IV Reign of Khufu." *Ornament* 14, no. 1.

———. 1996. "G7440Z and Boston's Bean-Net Dress." *KMT* 7, no.2 (summer 1996): 73–74.

Johnson, Sally B. 1990. *The Cobra Goddess of Ancient Egypt: Predynastic, Early Dynastic, and Old Kingdom Periods.* London and New York: Kegan Paul International.

Jones, Dilwyn. 2000. *An Index of Ancient Egyptian Titles, Epithets, and Phrases of the Old Kingdom.* 2 vols. Bar International Series 866. Oxford: Archaeopress.

Junge, Friedrich. 1995. "Hem-iunu, Anch-ha-ef und die sog. <Ersatzköpfe>." In *Kunst des Alten Reiches: Symposium im Deutschen Archäologischen Institut Kairo am 29. und 30. Oktober 1991,* 103–9. Sonderschrift des Deutsches Archäologisches Institut Abteilung Kairo 28. Mainz: Philipp von Zabern.

Junker, Hermann. 1929. *Die Mastabas der IV Dynastie auf dem Westfriedhof.* Vol. 1, *Giza.* Bericht über die von der Akademie der Wissenschaften in Wien auf gemeinsame Kosten mit Dr. Wilhelm Pelizaeus unternommenen Grabungen auf dem Friedhof des Alten Reiches bei den Pyramiden von Giza. Vienna and Leipzig: Hölder-Pichler-Tempsky A.G.

Kaiser, W. 1998. "Elephantine." In *Encyclopedia of Archaeology of Ancient Egypt,* ed. K. Bard, 283–89. London and New York: Routledge.

Kaplony, Peter. 1977. *Die Rollsiegel des Alten Reichs.* Brussels: Fondation égyptologique Reine Elisabeth.

———. 1981. *Die Rollsiegel des Alten Reichs II.* Brussels: Fondation égyptologique Reine Elizabeth.

———. 1983. "Rollseigel." In *Lexikon der Ägyptologie* 5, part 2, cols. 294–300. Wiesbaden: Otto Harrassowitz.

Keller, Cathleen A. 1995. "Stone Vessels and a Knife." In *The American Discovery of Ancient Egypt,* ed. Nancy Thomas, 120–21. Exh. cat. Los Angeles: Los Angeles County Museum of Art.

Killen, Geoffrey P. 1980. *Ancient Egyptian Furniture: 4000–1300 B.C.* Warminster: Aris and Phillips.

Krejčí, Jaromír. 2000. "The Origins and Development of the Royal Necropolis at Abusir during the Old Kingdom." In *Abusir and Saqqara in the Year 2000,* ed. Miroslav Bárta and Jaromír Krejčí, 467–84. Prague: Oriental Institute.

Krzyszkowska, Olga, and Morkot, Robert. 2000. "Ivory and Related Materials." In *Ancient Egyptian Materials and Technology,* ed. Paul Nicholson and Ian Shaw, 320–31. Cambridge: Cambridge University Press.

Labbé-Toutée, Sophie, and Christiane Ziegler. 1999. "Seked-Kaw, His Wife, and Their Son." In *Egyptian Art in the Age of the Pyramids,* 378–79. Exh. cat. New York: Metropolitan Museum of Art.

Lacovara, Peter. 1995a. "Funerary Furniture of Impy." In *The American Discovery of Ancient Egypt,* ed. Nancy Thomas, 137. Exh. cat. Los Angeles: Los Angeles County Museum of Art.

———. 1995b. "Menkaure." In *The American Discovery of Ancient Egypt,* ed. Nancy Thomas, 126. Exh. cat. Los Angeles: Los Angeles County Museum of Art.

———. 1997. "The Riddle of the Reserve Heads." *KMT* 8, no. 4 (winter):28–36.

Leclant, Jean. 1999. "A Brief History of the Old Kingdom." In *Egyptian Art in the Age of the Pyramids*, 3–11. Exh. cat. New York: The Metropolitan Museum of Art.

Lehmann, Katja. 1995. "Die Mastaba G 2009 auf dem Westfriedhof von Giza." Master's thesis, Universität Heidelberg.

Lehner, Mark. 1985. The *Pyramid Tomb of Hetep-heres and the Satellite Pyramid of Khufu*. Mainz: Philipp von Zabern.

———. 1997. *The Complete Pyramids: Solving the Ancient Mysteries*. London and New York: Thames and Hudson.

Leprohon, Ronald J. 1985. *Stelae I*. Corpus Antiquitatum Aegyptiacarum, Museum of Fine Arts, Boston, Fascicle 2. Mainz am Rhein: Philipp von Zabern.

Lichtheim, Miriam. 1973. *Ancient Egyptian Literature: A Book of Readings*. Vol. 1, *The Old and Middle Kingdoms*. Berkeley: University of California Press.

Lucas, Alfred. 1962. *Ancient Egyptian Materials and Industries*. 4th ed., rev. and enl. by John R. Harris. London: E. Arnold.

Maddin, R., T. Stech, J. D. Muhly, and E. Brovarski. 1984. "Old Kingdom Models from the Tomb of Impy: Metallurgical Studies." *Journal of Egyptian Archaeology* 70:33–41.

Málek, Jaromír. 1986. *In the Shadow of the Pyramids: Egypt during the Old Kingdom*. Norman, Okla.: University of Oklahoma Press.

Manniche, Lisa. 1991. *Music and Musicians in Ancient Egypt*. London: British Museum Press.

Manuelian, Peter Der. 1982. "Furniture." In *Egypt's Golden Age: The Art of Living in the New Kingdom, 1558–1085 B.C.*, ed. Edward Brovarski, Susan K. Doll, and Rita E. Freed, 63–66. Exh. cat. Boston: Museum of Fine Arts, Boston.

———. 1996. "March 1912: A Month in the Life of American Egyptologist George A. Reisner." *KMT* 7, no. 2 (summer):60–75.

———. 1998a. "A Case of Prefabrication at Giza? The False Door of Inty." *Journal of American Research Center in Egypt* 35:115–27.

———. 1998b. "The Problem of the Giza Slab Stelae." In *Stationen: Beiträge zur Kulturgeschichte Ägyptens: Festschrift für Rainer Stadelmann*, ed. Heike Guksch and Daniel Polz, 115–34. Mainz: Philipp von Zabern.

Markowitz, Yvonne. 1999. "Beaded Collars from the Old Kingdom in Ancient Egypt." *American Society of Jewelry Historians Newsletter* 13, no. 1 (spring):2–5.

Markowitz, Yvonne J., Joyce L. Haynes, and Peter Lacovara 2002. "The Silver Butterfly Bangles of Queen Hetepheres I." *Journal of American Research Center in Egypt*. Forthcoming.

Markowitz, Yvonne J., and Sheila B. Shear. 2001. "New Thoughts on an Old Egyptian Necklace: the Beaded Broadcollar of Ptahshepses Impy." *Adornment* 3, no. 2 (June–July):1–4.

Metropolitan Museum of Art. 1999. *Egyptian Art in the Age of the Pyramids*. New York: Metropolitan Museum of Art.

Millet, Nicholas B. 1999. "The Reserve Heads of the Old Kingdom: A Theory." In *Egyptian Art in the Age of the Pyramids*, 233–34. Exh. cat. New York: Metropolitan Museum of Art.

Moussa, Ahmed M., and Hartwig Altenmüller. 1977. *Das Grab des Nianchchnum und Chnumhotep*. Mainz am Rhein: Philipp von Zabern.

Müller, Hans Wolfgang, and Eberhard Thiem. 1999. *Gold of the Pharaohs*. Ithaca, N.Y.: Cornell University Press.

Münch, Hans-Hubertus. 2000. "Categorizing Archaeological Finds: the Funerary Material of Queen Hetepheres I at Giza." *Antiquity* 74:898–908.

Nicholson, Paul T., and Ian Shaw. 2000. *Ancient Egyptian Materials and Technology*. Cambridge: Cambridge University Press.

O'Connor, David. 1984. "Political Systems and Archaeological Data in Egypt: 2600–1780 B.C." *World Archaeology* 6:19–21.

Ogden, Jack. 2000. "Metals." In *Ancient Egyptian Materials and Technology*, ed. Paul Nicholson and Ian Shaw, 148–76. Cambridge: Cambridge University Press.

Otto, Eberhard. 1960. *Das ägyptische Mundöffnungsritual*. Ägyptologische Abhandlungen 3. Wiesbaden: Otto Harrassowitz.

Payne, Joan Crowfoot. 1993. *Catalogue of the Predynastic Egyptian Collection in the Ashmolean Museum*. Oxford: Griffith Institute.

Peterson, Bengt. 1986. "Finds from the Theteti Tomb at Saqqara." *Medelhavsmuseet Bulletin* 21:3–17.

Petrie, W. M. Flinders. 1903. *Abydos*. Part 2. London: Egypt Exploration Fund.

———. 1914. *Amulets*. London: Constable.

———. 1917. *Tools and Weapons Illustrated by the Egyptian Collection in University College, London, and 2000 Outlines from Other Sources*. London: British School of Archaeology in Egypt and Egyptian Research Account.

Pirelli, Rosanna. 1999. "Triad of Menkaure." In *Egyptian Treasures from the Egyptian Museum in Cairo*, ed. Francesco Tiradritti, 70–71. New York: Harry Abrams.

Porter, Bertha, and Rosalind L. B. Moss. 1937. *Topographical Bibliography of Ancient Egyptian Hieroglyphic Texts, Reliefs, and Paintings*. Vol. 5, *Upper Egypt: Sites*. Oxford: Clarendon Press.

———. 1974. *Topographical Bibliography of Ancient Egyptian Hieroglyphic Texts, Reliefs, and Paintings*. Vol. 3, *Memphis*. Part 1, *Abu Rawash to Abusir*. 2nd rev. ed. by Jaromír Málek. Oxford: Clarendon Press.

———. 1978. *Topographical Bibliography of Ancient Egyptian Hieroglyphic Texts, Reliefs, and Paintings*. Vol. 3.2, *Memphis*. Part 2, *Saqqara to Dashur*. 2nd rev. ed. by Jaromír Málek. Oxford: Clarendon Press.

———. 1981. *Topographical Bibliography of Ancient Egyptian Hieroglyphic Texts, Reliefs, and Paintings*. Vol. 3.2, *Memphis*. Part 2, *Saqqara to Dahshur*. 2nd ed. rev. by Jaromír Málek. Oxford: Clarendon Press.

Posener-Kriéger, Paule. 1976. *Les Archives du temple funéraire de Néferirkarê-Kakaï (Les papyrus d'Abousir): Traduction et commentaire*. 2 vols. Institut français d'archéologie orientale bibliothèque d'étude 65. Cairo: Institut français d'archéologie orientale.

Quibell, James Edward. 1909. *Excavations at Saqqara.* Vol. 2, *1906–1907.* Cairo: Institut français d'archéologie orientale.

———. 1913. *Excavations at Saqqara.* Vol. 5, *1911–1912: The Tomb of Hesy.* Cairo: Institut français d'archéologie orientale.

Quirke, Stephen. 1988. "Letter to the Dead." In *Mummies and Magic: The Funerary Arts of Ancient Egypt*, ed. Sue D'Auria, Peter Lacovara, and Catharine H. Roehrig, 106–7. Exh. cat. Boston: Museum of Fine Arts, Boston.

Ranke, Hermann. 1935. *Die ägyptischen Personennamen.* Vol. 1, *Verzeichnis der Namen.* Glückstadt: J. J. Augustin.

Reeder, Greg. 1993. "United for Eternity: Manicurists and Royal Confidents Niankhkhanum and Khanumhotep in Their Fifth-Dynasty Shared Mastaba-Tomb at Sakkara." *KMT* 4, no. 1 (spring):22–31.

Reisner, George A. n.d. a. Unpublished notes. Department of Art of the Ancient World, Museum of Fine Arts, Boston.

———. n.d. b. "A History of the Giza Necropolis I.2." Department of Art of the Ancient World, Museum of Fine Arts, Boston.

———. n.d. c. "Appendix L: A History of Cemetery 2000." Department of Art of the Ancient World, Museum of Fine Arts, Boston.

———. n.d. d. *Giza Diary 1909–1912.* Harvard University-Boston Museum of Fine Arts Egyptian Expedition Diary, Giza. Department of Art of the Ancient World, Museum of Fine Arts, Boston.

———. n.d. e. *Giza Diary 1912–1913.* Harvard University-Boston Museum of Fine Arts Egyptian Expedition Diary, Giza. Department of Art of the Ancient World, Museum of Fine Arts, Boston.

———. n.d. f. *Giza Necropolis 3.* Department of Art of the Ancient World, Museum of Fine Arts, Boston.

———. n.d. g. *Giza Object Register 1928–1930.* Harvard University-Boston Museum of Fine Arts Egyptian Expedition, Giza. Department of Art of the Ancient World, Museum of Fine Arts, Boston.

———. 1908. *The Early Dynastic Cemeteries of Naga-ed-Dêr.* Vol. 2. Part 1. Leipzig: J. C. Hinrichs.

———. 1911. "The Harvard University-Museum of Fine Arts Egyptian Expedition." *Museum of Fine Arts Bulletin* (Boston) 9, no. 50 (April):17–20

———. 1913. "New Acquisitions of the Egyptian Department: A Family of Builders of the Sixth Dynasty." *Museum of Fine Arts Bulletin* (Boston) 12, no. 66 (November): 53–66.

———. 1915. "Accessions to the Egyptian Department during 1914." *Museum of Fine Arts Bulletin* (Boston) 13, no. 76 (April):29–36.

———. 1927a. "Hetep-Heres, Mother of Cheops." *Museum of Fine Arts Bulletin* (Boston) 25, supplement (May):2–36.

———. 1927b. "The Tomb of Meresankh, a Great-Granddaughter of Queen Hetep-Heres and Sneferuw." *Museum of Fine Arts Bulletin* (Boston) 25, no. 151 (October):64–79.

———. 1931. *Mycerinus: The Temples of the Third Pyramid at Giza.* Cambridge, Mass.: Harvard University Press.

———. 1932a. "The Bed Canopy of the Mother of Cheops." *Museum of Fine Arts Bulletin* (Boston) 30, no. 180 (August): 56–60.

———. 1932b. *A Provincial Cemetery of the Pyramid Age, Naga-ed-Dêr.* Part 3. Oxford: University of California Publications.

———. 1936. *The Development of the Egyptian Tomb down to the Accession of Cheops.* Storrs-Mansfield, Conn.: Maurizio Martino.

———. 1942. *A History of the Giza Necropolis.* Vol. 1. Cambridge, Mass.: Harvard University Press.

Reisner, George A., and C. S. Fischer. 1911. "The Work of the Harvard University-Museum of Fine Arts Egyptian Expedition." *Museum of Fine Arts Bulletin* (Boston) 9, no. 50 (April):54–59.

Reisner, George A., and William Stevenson Smith. 1955. *A History of the Giza Necropolis.* Vol. 2, *The Tomb of Hetep-Heres the Mother of Cheops: A Study of Egyptian Civilization in the Old Kingdom.* Cambridge, Mass.: Harvard University Press.

Riefstahl, Elisabeth. 1956. "Two Hairdressers of the Eleventh Dynasty." *Journal of Egyptian Archaeology* 15:10–17.

Rigault, Patricia. 1999. "Necklace." In *Egyptian Art in the Age of the Pyramids*, 424. Exh. cat. New York: Metropolitan Museum of Art.

Roberts, David. 1995. "Age of Pyramids: Egypt's Old Kingdom." *National Geographic* 187 (January):2–43.

Robins, Gay. 1994. *Proportion and Style in Ancient Egyptian Art.* Austin: University of Texas Press.

———. 1997. *The Art of Ancient Egypt.* Cambridge, Mass.: Harvard University Press.

Roccati, Alessandro. 1986. "Uni." *Lexikon der Ägyptologie* 6, cols. 851–52. Wiesbaden: Otto Harrassowitz.

Roehrig, Catharine H. 1988. "Female Offering Bearer." In *Mummies and Magic: The Funerary Arts of Ancient Egypt*, ed. Sue D'Auria, Peter Lacovara, and Catharine H. Roehrig, 102–3. Exh. cat. Boston: Museum of Fine Arts, Boston.

———. 1999a. "Head of King Menkaure as a Young Man." In *Egyptian Art in the Age of the Pyramids*, 274–76. Exh. cat. New York: Metropolitan Museum of Art.

———. 1999b. "Mummy Mask and Body Covering." In *Egyptian Art in the Age of the Pyramids*, 476–77. Exh. cat. New York: Metropolitan Museum of Art.

———. 1999c. "Relief of Qar Hunting." In *Egyptian Art in the Age of the Pyramids*, 474–75. Exh. cat. New York: Metropolitan Museum of Art.

———. 1999d. "Reserve Head." In *Egyptian Art in the Age of the Pyramids*, 238–39. Exh. cat. New York: Metropolitan Museum of Art.

———. 1999e. "Reserve Heads: An Enigma of Old Kingdom Sculpture." In *Egyptian Art in the Age of the Pyramids*, 72–81. Exh. cat. New York: The Metropolitan Museum of Art.

Roth, Ann Macy. 1988a. "Mastaba Chapel of Akh-Meret-Nesut and his Family." In *Mummies and Magic: The Funerary Arts of Ancient Egypt*, ed. Sue D'Auria, Peter Lacovara, and Catharine H. Roehrig, 83–87. Exh. cat. Boston: Museum of Fine Arts, Boston.

———. 1988b. "Model Equipment with a *Pesesh-kef*." In *Mummies and Magic: The Funerary Arts of Ancient Egypt*, ed. Sue D'Auria, Peter Lacovara, and Catharine H. Roehrig, 81. Exh. cat. Boston: Museum of Fine Arts, Boston.

———. 1988c. "The Social Aspects of Death." In *Mummies and Magic: The Funerary Arts of Ancient Egypt*, ed. Sue D'Auria, Peter Lacovara, and Catharine H. Roehrig, 52–59. Exh. cat. Boston: Museum of Fine Arts, Boston.

———. 1988d. "Tomb Group of a Woman." In *Mummies and Magic: The Funerary Arts of Ancient Egypt*, ed. Sue D'Auria, Peter Lacovara, and Catharine H. Roehrig, 76–77. Exh. cat. Boston: Museum of Fine Arts, Boston.

———. 1991a. "The Distribution of the Old Kingdom Title Hnty-S." *Studien zur Altägyptischen Kultur*, no. 4:177–185.

———. 1991b. *Egyptian Phyles in the Old Kingdom: The Evolution of a System of Social Organization*. Studies in Ancient Oriental Civilization 48. Chicago: Oriental Institute of the University of Chicago.

———. 1992. "The *pesesh-kef* and the Opening of the Mouth." *Journal of Egyptian Archaeology* 78:112–48.

———. 1993. "Social Change in the Fourth Dynasty: The Spatial Organization of Pyramids, Tombs, and Cemeteries." *Journal of American Research Center in Egypt* 30:33–55.

———. 1995. *A Cemetery of Palace Attendants*. Giza Mastaba Series 6. Boston: Museum of Fine Arts, Boston.

———. 2001. Personal correspondence.

Russmann, Edna R. 1989. *Egyptian Sculpture: Cairo and Luxor*. Austin: University of Texas Press.

———. 1995. "A Second Style in Egyptian Art of the Old Kingdom." *Mitteilungen des Deutschen Archäologischen Instituts Abteilung Kairo* 51:269–79.

Rzepka, Slawomir. 2000. "One or two B3-b3.fs? Some Remarks on Two Old Kingdom Tombs at Giza." *Mitteilungen des Deutschen Archäologischen Instituts Abteilung Kairo* 56:353–60.

Saad, Zaki. 1969. *The Excavations at Helwan*. Norman, Okla.: University of Oklahoma Press.

Saleh, Mohammed, and Hourig Sourouzian. 1987. *The Egyptian Museum Cairo: Official Catalogue*. Mainz am Rhein: Philipp von Zabern.

Sanborn, Ashton. 1922. "Recent Acquisitions from Egypt." *Museum of Fine Arts Bulletin* (Boston) 20, no. 118 (April):25–27.

Schäfer, Heinrich. 1910. *Ägyptische Goldschmiedearbeiten*. Berlin: Verlag Von Karl Curtis.

———. 1974. *The Principles of Egyptian Art*. Rev., ed., and trans. John Baines. Oxford: Clarendon Press.

Scheel, Bernd. 1989. *Egyptian Metalworking and Tools*. Princes Risborough, Aylesbury Bucks, U.K.: Shire Publications.

Schorsch, D. 1992. "Copper Ewers of Early Dynastic and Old Kingdom Egypt—An Investigation of the Art of Smithing in Antiquity." *Mitteilungen des Deutschen Archäologischen Instituts Abteilung Kairo* 48:145–59.

Schulz, Regine, and Matthias Seidel, eds. 1998. *Egypt: The World of the Pharaohs*. Cologne: Köln.

Seidel, Matthias. 1996. *Pelizaeus Museum Hildesheim: The Egyptian Collection*. Mainz: Philipp von Zabern.

Seidelmayer, Stephan. 1998. "The Rise of the State to the Second Dynasty." In *Egypt: The World of the Pharaohs*, ed. Regine Schulz and Matthias Seidel, 24–39. Cologne: Köln.

Siliotti, Alberto. 1997. *Guide to the Pyramids of Egypt*. New York: Barnes and Noble.

Simpson, William Kelly. 1970. "A Late Old Kingdom Letter to the Dead from Nag' ed-Deir N 3500." *Journal of Egyptian Archaeology* 56:58–64.

———. 1976. *The Mastabas of Qar and Idu, G 7101 and 7102*. Giza Mastabas Series 2. Boston: Museum of Fine Arts, Boston.

———. 1977. *The Face of Egypt: Permanence and Change in Egyptian Art*. Katonah, N.Y.: Katonah Gallery.

———. 1978. *The Mastabas of Kawab, Khafkhufu I and II*. Giza Mastabas Series 3. Boston: Museum of Fine Arts, Boston.

———. 1980. *Mastabas of the Western Cemetery, Part I*. Giza Mastabas Series 4. Boston: Museum of Fine Arts, Boston.

Smith, Joseph Lindon. 1956. *Tombs, Temples, and Ancient Art*. Norman, Okla: University of Oklahoma Press.

Smith, William Stevenson. 1935. "The Old Kingdom Linen List." *Zeitschrift für ägyptische Sprache und Altertumskunde* 71:134–49.

———. 1936. "Topography of the Old Kingdom Cemetery at Saqqarah." Appendix C in *Development of the Egyptian Tomb Down to the Accession of Cheops*, by George A. Reisner, 390–411. Cambridge, Mass.: Harvard University Press.

———. 1942. "The Origin of Some Unidentified Old Kingdom Reliefs." *American Journal of Archaeology* 46:509–31.

———. 1946. *A History of Egyptian Sculpture and Painting in the Old Kingdom*. Boston: Oxford University Press.

———. 1958. *The Art and Architecture of Ancient Egypt*. Rev. ed. Harmondsworth and Baltimore: Penguin Books.

———. 1960. *Ancient Egypt as Represented in the Museum of Fine Arts, Boston*. Boston: Museum of Fine Arts, Boston.

———. 1981. *The Art and Architecture of Ancient Egypt*. 2nd rev. ed. by William Kelly Simpson. New York: Penguin Books.

———. 1998. *The Art and Architecture of Ancient Egypt*. Rev. and enl. by William Kelly Simpson. New Haven: Yale University Press.

Soukiassian, G., M. Wuttmann, and D. Schaad. 1990. "La Ville d'Ayn-Asil à Dakhla: état des recherches." *Bulletin de l'Institute français d'archaéologie orientale* 90:347–58.

Spencer, A. Jeffrey. 1980. *Early Dynastic Objects: Catalogue of Egyptian Antiquities in the British Museum*. Vol. 5. London: British Museum Publications.

Stadelmann, Rainer. 1997. "The Development of the Pyramid Temple in the Fourth Dynasty." In *The Temple in Ancient Egypt: New Discoveries and Recent Research*, ed. Stephen Quirke, 1–16. London: British Museum Press.

———. 1998. "Royal Tombs from the Age of the Pyramids." In *Egypt: The World of the Pharaohs*, ed. Regine Schulz and Matthias Seidel, 46–77. Cologne: Köln.

Staehelin, Elisabeth. 1966. *Untersuchungen zur ägyptischen Tracht im Alten Reich*. Münchner ägyptologische Studien 8. Berlin: Hessling.

Steindorff, Georg. 1937. "Ein Reliefbildnis des Prinzen Hemiun." *Zeitschrift für ägyptische Sprache und Altertumskunde* 73:120–21.

Strudwick, Nigel. 1985a. *The Administration of Egypt in the Old Kingdom: The Highest Titles and Their Holders*. London and Boston: Kegan Paul International.

———. 1985b. "Three Monuments of Old Kingdom Treasury Officials." *Journal of Egyptian Archaeology* 71:43–51, pl. 3.1.

———. 1985c. Review of *Die Rollsiegel des Alten Reichs*, by Peter Kaplony. *Journal of Egyptian Archaeology* 71 (Reviews Supplement):27–29.

Tacke, Nikolaus. 1996. "Die Entwicklung der Mumienmaske im Alten Reich." *Mitteilungen des Deutschen Archäologischen Instituts Abteilung Kairo* 52:307–336.

Tefnin, Roland. 1991. *Art et magie au temps des pyramides: L'énigma des têtes dites de "replacement."* Monumenta Aeyptiaca 5. Brussels: Fondation égyptologique Reine Elisabeth.

Thomas, Nancy. 1995. *The American Discovery of Ancient Egypt*. Exh. cat. Los Angeles: Los Angeles County Museum of Art.

Verner, Miroslav. 1985. "Les Sculptures de Rêneferef decouvertes à Abousir." *Bulletin de l'Institut français d'archéologie orientale* 85:267–80.

Ward, William. 1980. Review of *Die Rollsiegel des Alten Reichs*, by Peter Kaplony. *Bibliotheca Orientalis* 37:163-65.

Wenke, R., P. Buck, H. Hamroush, M. Kobusiewicz, K. Kroeper, and R. Redding. 1988. "Kom el-Hisn: Excavation of an Old Kingdom Settlement in the Egyptian Delta." *Journal of American Research Center in Egypt* 25:5–34.

Wilkinson, Alix. 1971. *Ancient Egyptian Jewellery*. London: Methuen.

Wilkinson, Richard H. 1994. *Symbol and Magic in Egyptian Art*. London: Thames and Hudson.

Wood, Wendy. 1974. "A Reconstruction of the Triads of King Mycerinus." *Journal of Egyptian Archaeology* 60:82–93.

Young, William J. 1972. "The Fabulous Gold of the Pactolus Valley." *Bulletin of the Museum of Fine Arts* (Boston) 70, no. 359:5–12.

Ziegler, Christiane. 1997. *Musée du Louvre, Département des antiquités égyptiennes: Les Statues égyptiennes de l'Ancien Empire*. Paris: Réunion des musées nationaux.

———. 1999a. "Jubilee Jar Inscribed with the Name of Pepi I." In *Egyptian Art in the Age of the Pyramids*, 448. Exh. cat. New York: Metropolitan Museum of Art.

———. 1999b. "Prince Ba-baef Standing." In *Egyptian Art in the Age of the Pyramids*, 298. Exh. cat. New York: Metropolitan Museum of Art.

———. 1999c. "The Statues of King Khafre." In *Egyptian Art in the Age of the Pyramids*, 252. Exh. cat. New York: Metropolitan Museum of Art.

Fig. 1
Line Drawing of King "Scorpion" on a limestone macehead, Dynasty 0. From Smith 1998, fig. 12.

Fig. 2
Colossal limestone statue of Min from Coptos, Dynasty 0. © 2001 The Ashmolean Museum, Oxford

Fig. 3
Schist statue of King Khasekhem, Dynasty 2. The Egyptian Museum, Cairo JE 32161. © 2001 Jürgen Liepe.

Fig. 4
The Step Pyramid of Kind Djoser at Saqqara, Dynasty 3. © 1999 Brian Snyder.

Fig. 5
The Bent Pyramid of King Sneferu at Dahshur, Dynasty 4. © 2001 Rita E. Freed.

Fig. 6
The pyramids at Giza, looking northwest, April 24, 1999. © 1999 Brian Snyder.

Fig. 7
Anorthosite gneiss statue of King Khafre with the Horus falcon, Dynasty 4. The Egyptian Museum, Cairo CG 14. © 2001 Victor R. Boswell, Jr., The National Geographic Society

Fig. 8
Greywacke statue of King Menkaure and a queen, Dynasty 4. Museum of Fine Arts, Boston 11.1738.

Fig. 9
Limestone figure of Hemiunu, Dynasty 4, reign of Khufu. © 1962 Roemer-und Pelizaeus-Museum, Hildesheim.

Fig. 10
Painted limestone bust of Prince Ankhhaf, Dynasty 4, reign of Khafre. Museum of Fine Arts, Boston 27.442.

Fig. 11
Painted limestone statuette of Ptahneferti as a child, Dynasty 5. Museum of Fine Arts, Boston 06.1881.

Fig. 12
Pleated linen dress from a woman's burial at Naga ed-Deir, Dynasty 6. Museum of Fine Arts, Boston 34.56.

Fig. 13
Agricultural relief scene from the offering chapel of Sekhemankhptah, Dynasty 5. Museum of Fine Arts, Boston 04.1760.

Fig. 14
Line drawing of the pull saw scene from the tomb of Ti at Saqqara, Dynasty 6. From Épron and Daumas 1939, 120.

Fig. 15
Boat jousting scene from the offering chapel of Sekhemankhptah, Dynasty 5. Museum of Fine Arts, Boston 04.1760.

Fig. 16
Limestone statuette of a seated man, Dynasty 6. Museum of Fine Arts, Boston 39.832.

Fig. 17
George Andrew Reisner, June 26, 1933.

Fig. 18
Line drawing of mastaba tomb construction by Suzanne Chapman for the Museum of Fine Arts, Boston.

Fig. 19
General view of the Western Cemetary, looking west, from the top of the Great Pyramid of Khufu, June 25, 1932.

Fig. 20
Painted limestone slab stela of Prince Wepemnofret, Dynasty 4, reign of Khufu. © 2001 Phoebe Apperson Hearst Museum of Anthropology, University of California at Berkeley 6-19825.

Fig. 21
Reserve heads at Harvard Camp, December 17, 1913.

Fig. 22
Line drawing of a cross section of a pyramid. From Lehner 1997, 16.

Fig. 23
Drawing: Map of the Giza necropolis, showing the pyramids and the Western and Eastern cemeteries. © 2001 Peter Der Manuelian.

Photo: Aerial view of the Giza plateau (Great Pyramid of Khufu in the foreground, with the pyramids of Khafre and Menkaure in the background), looking southwest, mid-20th century.

Fig. 24
Head from a colossal alabaster statue of King Menkaure in situ, April 14, 1907, and colossal alabaster statue of King Menkaure, Museum of Fine Arts, Boston 09.204.

Fig. 25
The discovery of the Menkaure Valley Temple triads, July 10, 1908, and triad of King Menkaure, the goddess Hathor, and the deified Hare nome, Museum of Fine Arts, Boston 09.200.

Fig. 26
The living room at Harvard Camp, 1934.

Fig. 27
Noel Wheeler excavating in the tomb of Queen Hetepheres I, July 22, 1926.

Fig. 28
Painting of the tomb chamber of Queen Hetepheres I as it appeared when first seen on March 8, 1925, by Joseph Linden Smith. Museum of Fine Arts, Boston 27.388.

Fig. 29
Removing the stone sarcophagus from the tomb of Queen Hetepheres I, April 17, 1927.

Fig. 30
Subterranean chamber in the tomb of Queen Meresankh III, May 8, 1927.

Fig. 31
Line drawing of Queen Hetepheres II and Queen Meresankh III in a boat from the east wall, main room, tomb of Meresankh III, by Suzanne Chapman for the Museum of Fine Arts, Boston.

Fig. 32
Limestone statue of Queens Hetepheres II and Meresankh III, Dynasty 4. Museum of Fine Arts, Boston 30.1456.

Fig. 33
Limestone Penmeru family grouping, Dynasty 5. Museum of Fine Arts, Boston 12.1484.

Fig. 34
Model of the Giza plateau (scale 1:2000), 1998. © 2001 Harvard University Semitic Museum, Cambridge, Massachusetts.

Fig. 35
Seated limestone statues of Prince Rahotep and Nofret, from Meidum, Dynasty 4, reign of King Sneferu. The Egyptian Museum, Cairo CG 3 and CG 4. © 2001 Jürgen Liepe.

Fig. 36
Relief scene featuring starving bedouins from the causeway of the pyramid of King Unas at Saqqara, Dynasty 5. Musée du Louvre, Paris E 17381. © 2001 Bruce White.

Fig. 37
Pyramid Texts from the antechamber of the pyramid of King Unas at Saqqara, Dynasty 5. © 2001 Victor R. Boswell, Jr., The National Geographic Society.

Fig. 38
Wooden figure of Meryrehaishetef, from Sedment, Dynasty 6, reign of King Pepy I. © 2001 Trustees of the British Museum, London EA 55722.

Fig. 39
Relief figure of the overseer of all works, Nekhebu, Dynasty 6. Museum of Fine Arts, Boston 13.4335.

Cat. no. 1
The entrance to Queen Hetepheres I's tomb in the area east of the Great Pyramid, 1925 or 1926.

Line drawing from the mastaba of Queen Meresankh III showing a bedmaking under a canopy. From Dunham and Simpson 1974, fig. 8.

Cat. no. 2
Line drawing of craftsmen in the pottery workshop of Ti at Saqqara. Adapted by Elizabeth Simpson after Épron and Daumas 1939, pl. 71.

Cat. no. 5
Pyramid complex of King Menkaure. From Lehner 1997, 137.

Cat. no. 7
Alabaster statuary fragments of King Menkaure found in a drain hole outside the king's pyramid temple, April 14, 1907.

Cat. no. 8
Three of the unfinished statues of King Menkaure found in the Menkaure Valley Temple, 1908.

Cat. no. 16
Wrapped mummy of a woman from tomb G 2220 B.

Cat. no. 20
Seated statue of Akhmeretnesut in situ, April 12, 1912.

Cat. no. 21
Drawing of the decree of Neferirkare. © 2001 Peter Der Manuelian.

Cat. no. 22
Line drawing of a relief from the pyramid temple of King Sahure at Abusir of a person holding a cylinder seal. From Borchardt 1913, pl. 53.

Line drawing of the cylinder seal. From Kaplony 1981, pl. 92, no. 38.

Cat. no. 24
Drawing of the false door of Inty. © 2001 Peter Der Manuelian.

Cat. no. 25
Reconstruction drawing of the serdab in front of the mastaba of Babaef. From Arnold 1994, 235.

Cat. no. 28
Seated statue of Nyshepsesnesut in the serdab of the offering chamber, December 24, 1915.

Cat. no. 29
Intact statue grouping from the tomb of Weri, Summer 1920.

Cat. no. 31
Line drawing of a relief from the tomb of Djaty featuring the daughters of the deceased making bread, bearing offerings, and brewing beer. From Simpson 1980, pl. 41.

Cat. no. 32
Offering basin of Khnumu in situ (upside down in the foreground), 1905 or 1906.

Cat. no. 33
Canopic jars in the burial chamber, February 6, 1927.

Cat. no. 36
Drawing of the second chair from the tomb of Queen Hetepheres I. From Reisner and Smith 1955, fig. 32.

Cat. no. 38
Ornaments of Pthashepses Impy as they appeared on the body when the coffin was first opened, January 3, 1913.

Cat. no. 39
The burial chamber of Ptahshepses Impy as seen from the entranceway, December 3, 1912.

Cat. no. 41
Line drawing of the sculptor Inkaf working on a statue of Queen Meresankh III from the main chamber of the queen's mastaba. He holds a rectangular chisel in his right hand. From Dunham and Simpson 1974, fig. 5.

Cat. no. 44
The complete false door of Senwehem in situ, September 29, 1913.

Stela and bust of Idu, west wall, tomb of Idu (G 7102), January 17, 1925.

Six standing statues in a niche of Qar's tomb with a carved inscription above providing his name and chief titles, November 29, 1925.

Cat. no. 48
Line drawing of the pattern and bodice line of beads as described by excavator Noel Wheeler and used in the reconstruction of the beadnet dress. © 2001 Yvonne J. Markowitz.

Cat. no. 55
Hieroglyphic text from the letter to the dead from Naga ed-Deir. From Simpson 1970, pl. 46A.

MAP CREDITS:

p. 14
Map of Egypt with ancient sites and modern cities. © 2001 Peter Der Manuelian.

p. 15
Detail plan of the Western Cemetery at Giza showing the different excavation concessions of 1902–1953. © 2001 Peter Der Manuelian.

Designed by Cynthia Rockwell Randall

Edited by Emiko K. Usui and Sarah E. McGaughey

Typeset in Sabon and Frutiger

Printed and bound at Arnoldo Mondadori,

A.M.E. Publishing Ltd., Verona, Italy